*Religious Diversity
and University Chaplaincy*

Religious Diversity and University Chaplaincy

MUSLIM, HINDU, BUDDHIST, AND HUMANIST
CHAPLAINCY IN HIGHER EDUCATION

Gregory W. McGonigle

Foreword by Eboo Patel

☙PICKWICK *Publications* · Eugene, Oregon

RELIGIOUS DIVERSITY AND UNIVERSITY CHAPLAINCY
Muslim, Hindu, Buddhist, and Humanist Chaplaincy in Higher Education

Copyright © 2024 Gregory W. McGonigle. All rights reserved. Except for brief quotations in critical publications or reviews, no part of this book may be reproduced in any manner without prior written permission from the publisher. Write: Permissions, Wipf and Stock Publishers, 199 W. 8th Ave., Suite 3, Eugene, OR 97401.

Pickwick Publications
An Imprint of Wipf and Stock Publishers
199 W. 8th Ave., Suite 3
Eugene, OR 97401

www.wipfandstock.com

PAPERBACK ISBN: 978-1-6667-3820-9
HARDCOVER ISBN: 978-1-6667-9858-6
EBOOK ISBN: 978-1-6667-9859-3

Cataloguing-in-Publication data:

Names: McGonigle, Gregory W., author. | Patel, Eboo, foreword.

Title: Religious diversity and university chaplaincy : Muslim, Hindu, Buddhist, and humanist chaplaincy in higher education / Gregory W. McGonigle ; foreword by Eboo Patel.

Description: Eugene, OR : Pickwick Publications, 2024 | Includes bibliographical references and index.

Identifiers: ISBN 978-1-6667-3820-9 (paperback) | ISBN 978-1-6667-9858-6 (hardcover) | ISBN 978-1-6667-9859-3 (ebook)

Subjects: LCSH: Chaplains. | Religious pluralism—United States.

Classification: BV4011.3 .M335 2024 (print) | BV4011.3 .M335 (ebook)

With love and gratitude for my sister,
Lisa Savilia.

Contents

Foreword ix

Acknowledgments xiii

Introduction 1

1 Muslim Chaplaincy 11
2 Hindu Chaplaincy 30
3 Buddhist Chaplaincy 53
4 Humanist Chaplaincy 85
5 Conclusion 119

Appendix I: Chaplains Interviewed 125

About the Author 127

Bibliography 129

Index 135

Foreword

HERE ARE SOME STATISTICS that might get your attention: there are as many Muslims in the United States as there are ELCA Lutherans, and approximately twice as many Buddhists as Episcopalians. Perhaps even more striking: the median age of Buddhists and Muslims is twenty years younger than the median age of Lutherans and Episcopalians.

Moreover, those communities are far from homogenous. American Muslims and American Buddhists are big tent communities that contain variants of literally every sect of Islam and school of Buddhism on the planet. The same can be said of Hindus, Daoists, Sikhs, Confucians, Pagans, and on and on and on.

The most religiously diverse nation in human history is about to become even more complex in matters of faith.

As David French reminds us in his book, *Divided We Fall*, religious diversity has long led to not just division but to ugly prejudice and outright conflict. We in the United States have seen our fair share of this, from the anti-Catholic Know Nothing movement of the mid-19th century, to the cross burnings of the KKK in the 1920s, to the January 6th insurrection, which was suffused with the symbols of white Christian nationalism.

And yet, as French points out, the United States by and large has a better record on matters of religious diversity than on any other dimension of identity, certainly race or gender or sexuality. No doubt this has much to do with the north star set by the European Founders of the 1776 generation.

With the harrowing experience of the European Wars of Religion fresh in their minds, the flawed group of white men who created the U.S. Constitutional framework (Washington, Madison, Adams, Jefferson, Franklin and Hamilton) somehow managed to establish a system that allowed for the free expression of diverse religions while also protecting the republic from undue influence by any particular faith. It is a genius solution to a problem that has destroyed more kingdoms, nations and empires than one could count.

That constitutional framework combined with the leadership of presidents ranging from Abraham Lincoln to Barack Obama, and the example of civic institutions like Hull House and the NCCJ, has allowed the flourishing of religiously diverse democracy in the United States. But as we look at the religious dimensions of American diversity, and the diversity dimensions of American religion, the question presents itself: will we go from strength to strength when it comes to interfaith issues, or will we succumb to the same prejudice and conflict that has felled earlier civilizations?

In this work, Greg McGonigle offers us clear reasons for hope. On college campuses across the country, leaders of different faiths have gathered in university chaplaincy programs, not just to support their own communities, but to nurture a new generation in appreciative knowledge of diverse faiths and to teach the skills of interfaith leadership.

Colleges, as Professor Andy DelBanco of Columbia University reminds us, are among the jewels of American civilization. Over half of America's private colleges were founded by religious communities. This includes seven of the eight Ivy League schools, over two hundred Catholic colleges and 120 campuses founded by Methodists, including prominent institutions like Emory, Duke, Syracuse and USC.

For decades, these institutions have admitted students from all faith persuasions. Indeed, I am in this country because a university founded by French Catholic priests on the Indiana prairie, built principally for the uplift of poor midwestern Catholic boys, found fit to admit a wayward Ismaili Muslim international student from India to its MBA program in the mid-1970s. That university is Notre Dame and that man was my father. I am literally Fighting Irish from birth.

Notre Dame, like so many Catholic universities, now has active Muslim and Jewish organizations on campus. They tend to the religious and cultural needs of the growing Muslim and Jewish populations at the university, and encourage them in interfaith efforts. The same, as McGonigle documents, is happening at dozens of other universities across the country, with some universities taking the lead to intentionally include religious diversity on their professional staffs.

Some of these students will be inspired to become spiritual leaders in their faiths, and will undoubtedly continue their interfaith leadership beyond campus. Most will likely pursue other professions – medicine,

Foreword

diplomacy, business, law. They will know from their university experience that faith can be a bridge of cooperation and not a barrier of division. They will bring into tech companies and government agencies the interfaith friendships and perspective-taking skills they learned on campus.

They will help the United States move beyond its current conception of itself as a Judeo-Christian country, and embrace an even more hopeful, inclusive, and forward-looking narrative: Interfaith America.

Eboo Patel
January 2024

Acknowledgments

I AM DEEPLY GRATEFUL to all of those who have made this book possible, beginning with my whole family, as well as my main mentors in the field of university chaplaincy and ministry in higher education, The Rev. Janet Cooper Nelson and the late Rev. Professor Peter J. Gomes.

I am grateful to Professor Diana Eck and the Harvard Pluralism Project, who instilled in me a passion for studying religious diversity in the United States, as a way of helping to promote religious literacy, interfaith engagement, peace and social justice. And I am grateful to all of my teachers and mentors at Brown, Harvard, and Boston University. Especially at BU, I am grateful to my thesis readers and reviewers Dean Robert Allan Hill, Dean Mary Elizabeth Moore, IRB reviewer Professor Nancy Ammerman, and program director Dr. Eileen Daily. And I am grateful to the team at Wipf and Stock Publishers for making this book a reality.

I am deeply grateful to so many I have worked and served with who shaped my journey, including those at St. Paul's School, the Boston Living Center, Dana Farber Cancer Institute, the UU Church of Davis, the UU Legislative Ministry of California, the University of California at Davis, Oberlin College, Tufts University, and Emory University. The students of the UC Davis, Oberlin, Tufts, and Emory interfaith student councils and the Tufts CAFÉ and Emory WISE pre-Orientation programs have also deeply informed my perspective on interfaith work.

I am grateful to my senior colleagues and advisors, including Edward Schreiber, The Rev. Walter Moczynski, The Rev. Elizabeth Banks, The Rev. Lindi Ramsden, Dean Linda Gates, Dean Eric Estes, Michael Baenen, President Anthony Monaco, President Claire Sterk, and President Gregory Fenves.

Acknowledgments

Dear friends who have supported me, taught me, and shaped my thought in the fields of ministry, chaplaincy, and higher education leadership are too many to name, but they include The Rev. Erika Hewitt and The Rev. Patty Franz; The Revs. Mary and Steve Hammond and Professor Mohammad J. Mahallati; Dean Mary Pat McMahon; and Tufts chaplaincy colleagues The Rev. Daniel Bell, Rabbi Naftali Brawer, Chaplain Walker Bristol, Shelby Carpenter, Alex Chiu, Dr. Lynn Cooper, Dr. Celene Ibrahim, Linda Karpowich, Ven. Upali Sraman, and Rabbi Jeffrey Summit.

Cherished colleagues adjacent to this work who have supported me and influenced my thoughts include Dr. Eboo Patel and Rabbi Or Rose.

And I am grateful to so many current Emory colleagues, including Provost Ravi Bellamkonda, Dr. Robert Franklin, Dean Enku Gelaye, Dr. Carol Henderson, and Dr. Anjulet Tucker, as well as our chaplaincy team Maury Allums, Rabbi Jordan Braunig, Brni. Shweta Chaitanya, Zachary Cole, The Rev. Maddie Henderson Herlong, Lakishia Hines, Liz Martin, Sara McKlin, Ven. Priya Rakkhit Sraman, Dr. Isam Vaid and our affiliates.

Friends who have kept me going and encouraged me along the way include Chandra Glick, Howard and Doris Hunter, and Loc Truong.

I am grateful to the professional associations in which I have been involved, especially the National Association of College and University Chaplains (NACUC), the Association for College and University Religious Affairs (ACURA), and now the Association for Chaplains and Spiritual Life in Higher Education (ACSLHE) as well as the International Association of Chaplains in Higher Education (IACHE).

I am grateful to my spiritual communities, including the First Unitarian Church of Providence, First Parish in Cambridge, Arlington Street Church, Harvard Divinity School, The Memorial Church at Harvard, Follen UU Church in Lexington, Mass., and the UU Congregation of Atlanta.

And finally, I am grateful to all the colleagues and fellow travelers who allowed me to interview them and base this study on their thoughts—you enrich and bless us all.

Introduction

OVER THE PAST TWENTY years of my career in higher education—as an undergraduate, a divinity student, a campus minister, and now a university chaplain and dean of religious life—the religious and philosophical demographics of students on college and university campuses in the United States have been changing dramatically. When I matriculated at Brown University in the late 1990s, it was in part because of my own religious developments—I had been brought up in a Catholic family, and I chose to attend a Catholic high school to be able to study religion in school. Studying the Bible from the historical critical approach raised many questions for me about my faith, however, while studying American literature introduced me to Transcendentalist authors like Ralph Waldo Emerson and Henry David Thoreau, whose philosophical themes rooted in the New England region in which I grew up shaped my adolescent mind and values. Their encouragement to seek self-reliance, to pursue firsthand experiences with God, to revere the natural world and the interdependence of life, to work to improve society for the common good, and to appreciate spiritual paths from around the world all became themes that shaped my own religious worldview as I became a young adult.

I went to Brown because I had learned a bit about religions other than Christianity and I wanted to study them in greater depth, and I also wanted to do so in a diverse environment that gave me considerable freedom in the classroom and in my cocurricular life, especially as I began to become more liberal politically and to understand myself as a gay man. Through studies of religions and making new friends at Brown, I began to witness the increasing religious diversity of the United States—Brown was not all Protestant, Catholic, and Jewish like the Massachusetts town in which I had grown up; my classmates were also Muslim, Hindu, Buddhist, and Humanist, and indeed there were many who were simply spiritual or did not claim any religious affiliation at all.

Religious Diversity and University Chaplaincy

Although, at that time, Brown already had a number of diverse religious student organizations, there was no one group where students of different faiths came together to dialogue and share about their faiths with one another. Therefore, working with Brown's university chaplain, The Rev. Janet Cooper Nelson, and the Brown Office of the Chaplains and Religious Life, my friends and I formed the Brown Multifaith Council. The Rev. Cooper Nelson was already known for supporting religious diversity in American higher education, and she became our advisor, hosting us for meetings and retreats about interfaith engagement.

My interest in these activities was also fueled by the work of Harvard University Professor Diana Eck, whose Pluralism Project was beginning to document the changing religious landscape of Boston and later the United States. The Pluralism Project began to illustrate how this shifting landscape was changing the faith traditions present as well as the civic lives of communities. In addition to its research, the project promoted the idea of *religious pluralism*—defined as active engagement with religious diversity in order to build understanding, reduce stereotypes, and foster civic cohesion. Reading Professor Eck's work so interested me that I applied to lead a group independent study course in the Brown religious studies department, with the goal of adding an opportunity to study contemporary U.S. "lived religion" and how religions were interacting with one another.

In the course, "World Religions in America," we studied the historical development of religions in the United States, starting with Native Peoples' traditions, and with a special focus on the post-1965 New Immigration and the growing presence of religions such as Islam, Hinduism, and Buddhism in the U.S. For our final group project, we began studying newer religious communities locally in Rhode Island, literally mapping and collecting the histories of the first mosques, Sikh gurdwaras, Buddhist centers, and other non-Christian and non-Jewish spiritual centers in Rhode Island.

Most of my undergraduate degree in religious studies had been focused on South Asian religions, but after learning about the Pluralism Project and its potential for connecting religion and with the social ethic of advancing a more pluralistic society, I became increasingly interested in studying contemporary American religious history. At the same time, my personal faith and social justice commitments developed, and I began to discern a vocation to become a Unitarian Universalist minister and a university chaplain. I was accepted to Harvard Divinity School, and I was

INTRODUCTION

excited to continue studying religions at one of the most religiously diverse divinity schools in the country.

In my very first days there, the tragedy of September 11, 2001 took place in New York, and soon after that, the initial reports of hate crimes against Muslims, Sikhs, and Hindus in its aftermath. It was clear to me that a new era of interfaith learning and engagement would be needed in order to build mutual understanding and promote the values of human dignity, respect, equality, justice, compassion, community, and peace.

Through my studies, I continued to focus on this reality of increasing religious diversity and interaction, and I began to work as a researcher for the Harvard Pluralism Project, continuing and developing the research I had begun on world religions in Rhode Island while at Brown. Through ministerial internships, I witnessed the new religious landscape taking shape in Boston in the populations of the public health centers and hospitals where I interned, and I continued to see this after graduation as well, when I became a campus minister at the University of California at Davis.

From Student to Chaplain

After a congregational internship in the UU Church of Davis, my first ministry position was at a progressive Protestant campus ministry at UC Davis that was responding to 9/11 with a multifaith project—converting a parcel of its land into a multifaith living community for forty students of different faiths to live together, learn, and build friendships. I was hired in part to help develop this campus ministry's relationships with our multifaith partners—the Hillel center, the Newman Catholic center, a Lutheran Episcopal campus ministry, and the new mosque next door. My work at UC Davis also involved serving on interfaith councils and engaging in various interfaith initiatives, and I learned a great deal more there about religious diversity and interaction.

After three years, I felt called to lead and develop my own multifaith college chaplaincy program, and I was hired as the first multifaith director of the Office of Religious and Spiritual Life at Oberlin College. With this charge, it was my responsibility to support the full religious diversity of the college, including many students who were atheist, agnostic, nonreligious, and spiritual but not religious. During this time, Eboo Patel had founded the organization Interfaith Youth Core in order to make interfaith engagement a more widespread social norm through consulting with colleges and universities. He began working with President Barack Obama to deepen interfaith relations and developed a White House Interfaith Challenge. Getting involved in that challenge encouraged us at Oberlin to form an Interfaith Student Council that became the launchpad for many interfaith initiatives, such as interfaith community service internships and annual interfaith days of service. We also partnered with other campus offices on multicultural initiatives, opened a new Multifaith Center space, and began to explore interreligious and interfaith studies more deeply through a course I taught on interfaith leadership. Additionally, we formalized the college's first Muslim chaplain position, hosted events with artists and speakers from underrepresented traditions on Oberlin's campus like Hinduism and developed a thriving Buddhist meditation program.

In 2013, I left Oberlin College for Tufts University, attracted by Tufts' Universalist heritage and its embrace of a robust model of university chaplaincy to serve the whole university through a team of several staff chaplains of different faiths, which was put in place by a predecessor, The Rev Scotty McLennan. When I arrived, Tufts had four chaplains in addition to my position. These chaplains were Protestant, Catholic, Jewish, and Muslim, and all worked for the university and shared in interfaith duties.

But not all students felt served—for several years, Tufts had had a strong and growing Humanist community (called the Freethought Society) that had connections with the Harvard Humanist Hub. These students and their alumni supporters desired to have a Humanist chaplain at Tufts. In addition, the Tufts Buddhist Mindfulness Sangha meditation community had been served by several volunteer advisors over time but had never had a paid professional chaplain to lead regular meditation sessions and develop other Buddhist programs and a deeper community.

Similarly, the Africana Protestant community had had a Black Theology Bible study for several years, but they desired to be more connected with the university chaplaincy and have more official support. And Tufts had a sizeable community of Hindus and practitioners of other South Asian religions, who saw other universities like Harvard and MIT that had Hindu affiliates in their chaplaincies. The success and vibrancy of the chaplaincy programs with the communities that did have professional chaplains generated a desire for chaplaincy support from many of these student constituencies and communities. And so, over my years at Tufts, we were able to add chaplain or advisor positions to our staff for each of these communities. These colleagues and our collective work began to have a strong impact on

INTRODUCTION

the campus community—reaching beyond spiritual life to support many current university priorities such as diversity and inclusion, wellness, and civic engagement.

This story, and that of the other universities that have been making this journey toward increasing the religious diversity of their university chaplaincy programs, presents the central questions of this book: How have college and university chaplaincies and spiritual life programs been adapting to serve the increasing religious diversity of the United States? In universities where chaplain positions have been added for traditions beyond Christianity and Judaism, how have these positions come to be? For the new chaplains who have taken on these roles, what kind of preparation did they have, and what do they feel they needed? What have been the shapes of the programs they developed, and what have been their main successes and challenges? Additionally, how do these chaplains from newer traditions to U.S. higher education see the future of their traditions and of their work in our new and changing spiritual landscape? And what might that suggest about the religiously diverse and interfaith reality growing in the U.S.?

Responding to a Changing Landscape

This book addresses the fact that the religious and philosophical diversity of American colleges and universities has increased dramatically over the past thirty years, and in many cases, university chaplaincies have not kept pace in terms of the number and types of chaplain positions universities have. Most universities and colleges in the United States that have chaplaincies or offices of religious and spiritual life were founded by Protestants or Catholics, and for most of their histories they have tended to have chaplains of their own traditions serving their campuses.

With the increasing numbers of Catholics and Jews attending Protestant institutions in the last century, many universities added chaplains, chaplaincies, or campus ministries to serve Catholic and Jewish students. However, with the increasing diversity of students who are the children of the post-1965 New Immigration to the U.S. of people from the Middle East, South Asia, and East Asia, who may be practitioners of Islam, Hinduism, Buddhism, and other traditions, many American universities have not yet added chaplains to represent and serve students of these traditions.

At the same time, there is a growing number of students who identify as Humanist, atheist, agnostic, nonreligious, or spiritual but not religious, who may have spiritual needs that are beyond the scope of traditional religion. At a number of institutions, these students have been shown to have a desire for many of the resources and supports that chaplaincies have traditionally provided—spaces of caring community; opportunities for meditation, reflection, and counseling; educational spaces to consider life's big questions; and pathways to engage in meaningful service and social justice work. There are several campuses where innovative programs to meet the emerging needs of Humanists or of the "spiritual but not religious" have developed, but they are not yet widespread or widely recognized, documented, and supported.

For educational leaders who would seek to consider developing more diverse spiritual life programs or for students who desire and would seek to advocate for them, very little research currently exists on the development of chaplaincies from these historically underrepresented traditions. The current knowledge regarding the diversification of university chaplaincies mostly exists in the stories of the chaplain leaders who have begun to develop these programs as positions have become needed and been created; however, this knowledge has not been comprehensively documented. The purpose of this book is to collect and share some of these stories in a way that will encourage more university communities to consider diversifying their spiritual life programs based on how this has occurred on different campuses in different contexts.

To explore and present some of the diversity and texture of these stories, I interviewed at least three chaplains of each of these emerging traditions in university chaplaincy in the U.S.—Islam, Hinduism, Buddhism, and Humanism—chaplains who themselves represent different personal backgrounds, different types of institutions, and different regions of the country. Through the stories of how their positions developed, how they came into them, what their work looks like, their achievements and challenges, and their visions for the future, they depict the increasing religious and spiritual diversity of U.S. university campuses and they reveal the benefits that the development of spiritual life programs to reflect and support this diversity can have to the university overall.

How Did We Get Here?

The field of university chaplaincy for Muslims, Hindus, Buddhists, Humanists, and other historically underrepresented religious and philosophical communities in the United States is a growing field but, in most cases, it is still very much in its beginnings. To date, these communities lack a great deal of the infrastructure and support that has been built around Protestant, Catholic, and Jewish university religious life over the past centuries and decades. Historically, the oldest universities and colleges in the United States were founded by Protestants, and often had faculty or staff positions for (Protestant) chaplains or developed them in early years. Later, new waves of immigration and changes in policies led to increasing numbers of Catholics and Jews entering American higher education, and those communities developed ways to supplement the Protestant religious life of universities—often through the development of Newman Catholic centers and Hillel and other Jewish centers—over the past hundred years.

But a similar structure has yet to develop for the growing number of Muslims on today's university campuses, and except in very few cases, Hindu, Buddhist, and Humanist communities are further behind on such support. Student organizations for these communities often exist and occasionally have volunteer advisors, but without the larger networks, structures, and funding that other traditions have developed, it is difficult to employ the professional chaplaincy staff members who are vital to providing high-quality and effective university religious and philosophical life.

Surveying the Field Today

Much like the increasingly multireligious landscape of the United States before the work of the Harvard Pluralism Project, the diversification of university and college chaplaincy along multireligious lines remains largely an untold story. The microhistories of the development of Muslim, Hindu, Buddhist, and Humanist chaplaincies in higher education mostly remain embedded in personal narratives of those who have created and the chaplains who have stepped into these roles. In addition, not much analysis has been done about the development of these new chaplaincies, and this may contribute to the difficulty of developing them and hinder advocacy for them where they do not exist.

I have been fortunate in my career as a director of religious life, university chaplain, and dean of religious life to have been connected with many of those who have helped to move forward the diversification of college and university religious life to date and also those who have begun to occupy these new roles serving historically underrepresented traditions. This has been invaluable as I have worked to expand the spiritual life offerings and programs at the colleges and universities I have served.

The networks offered by the national professional associations of college and university chaplains have been critical to this developing work. Having served as past president of the National Association of College and University Chaplains (NACUC) and a board member in the Association for College and University Religious Affairs (ACURA)—two organizations that merged to form the Association for Chaplaincy and Spiritual Life in Higher Education (ACSLHE) in 2021—I came to know and learn from others leading university religious life and from those serving particular religious communities. These collegial networks, who have become my close friends in chaplaincy, provided the foundation for the research in this book.

Longtime colleagues as well as newer friends in this work, many of them regarded as national leaders, were generous enough to allow me to interview them and to learn more about their stories, their experiences, their insights, their challenges, and their visions for the future. I hope that my research will support them in their work and all of us who are interested in university spiritual life by encouraging universities to consider the benefits of expanding their spiritual life programs to incorporate historically underrepresented religious traditions in the United States.

Contents and Contexts

The structure of this book includes one chapter each on the development of university chaplaincy in the following traditions: Islam, Hinduism, Buddhism, and Humanism. These tradition-specific chapters are followed by a conclusion that summarizes and explores features both that are unique to these traditions and that cut across all of the traditions. Among these are the university structural issues that have allowed for or have hindered the development of university chaplaincies in the traditions I studied, including issues of institutional resources such as university administration support and personnel and program budgets.

Multireligious university chaplaincies have tended to develop at larger universities that are private, historically Protestant, have comparatively more resources than other schools, and have greater religious demographic diversity. However, these schools have become a bellwether for others, including smaller colleges, religiously-affiliated colleges, and even public

INTRODUCTION

universities that are all responding to the increasing religious diversity on campus and in the United States in various ways. This research holds insights for these contexts as well.

Opening New Pathways

I hope this book makes an important contribution to the field of university and college chaplaincy and higher education in general by documenting these new and important chaplaincy histories, identifying trends in the development of religiously diverse chaplaincies, allowing for best practices to be highlighted and shared, and providing resources for universities to consider the diversification of their chaplaincies and spiritual life programs.

What we think of and call "university chaplaincy" has changed a great deal over time in different eras, and so these new stories describe a new moment in the development of the field of university chaplaincy and spiritual life. I have sought to honor the work of the innovative colleagues who have led efforts to diversify the spiritual life resources on their university campuses, and the colleagues from the newer traditions to American university chaplaincy who are doing and developing this work today, in ways that I hope will open new pathways for others to join us in the future.

1

Muslim Chaplaincy

History

WHERE UNIVERSITIES AND COLLEGES have expanded their chaplaincies beyond the Protestant, Catholic, and Jewish traditions, the first position added has usually been that of a Muslim chaplain. As described by Yale University's first and current Muslim chaplain Omer Bajwa, the beginnings of Muslim chaplaincy in the United States were with Muslim prison chaplains associated with the Nation of Islam during the 1950s and 1960s, which famously led to Malcom X's conversion to Islam.[1] There was further development in the 1970s and 1980s, especially in hospital chaplaincy, and later the first Muslim chaplain in the U.S. armed forces in 1994.[2] A year earlier, Diana Chapman Walsh, who was then president of Wellesley College, hired Wellesley's dean of religious and spiritual life, The Rev. Victor Kazanjian, to begin serving the diverse spiritual life of the college by instituting a multifaith chaplaincy model that included the appointment of Wellesley College's first Muslim chaplain in 1993.[3] Howard University followed in 1994 and Georgetown in 1999, but a watershed moment that all of the Muslim chaplains I interviewed described was September 11, 2001, when, as Bajwa said, "the field took off in a major way."[4]

As Bajwa shared, September 11, 2001 caused allies of the Muslim community in university administrations, such as presidents, provosts,

---

1. Omer Bajwa, interview with author, November 24, 2020.
2. Kappler, "Chaplain Recalls Path to Making History."
3. Kazanjian, "Journey Toward Multi-Faith Community."
4. Omer Bajwa, interview with author, November 24, 2020.

university chaplains, and deans of campus life, to realize that the Muslim populations on U.S. university and college campuses had grown, and the structures of campus chaplaincies had in most cases not developed to support this new religious reality.[5] The administrations realized this because Muslim students, faculty, and staff were reaching out for support, and others on campus were seeking to learn more and support the Muslim community or were responding in ways that were Islamophobic.[6]

It became clear that Muslim students (and faculty and staff) on campus were not well supported, and universities needed more religious life staff with greater specific expertise.[7] Beyond addressing the immediate spiritual and pastoral care needs of Muslim students, faculty, and staff, such as Friday prayers, Ramadan and Eid observances, etc., this work involved assessing campus climates to ensure that campuses were hospitable to Muslim students, faculty, and staff, with resources such as prayer space, ablution rooms, halal food, iftars and *suhur* meals during Ramadan, and other such needs.[8] In addition, the two divergent reactions that September 11 elicited in the non-Muslim population—one of prejudice and discrimination, and another of a desire to learn more about Islam and build positive interfaith relationships—meant that Muslim chaplains were needed to help with stereotype and prejudice reduction, campus education, and the building of interfaith relationships.[9]

Responding to these needs, more universities began to add Muslim chaplain positions, such as NYU in 2005, Brown and Princeton in 2006, Tufts in 2007, Duke and Yale in 2008, Northwestern in 2010, and Cornell and Harvard in 2017.[10] Many of these positions began with a graduate student, faculty member, or staff member serving in a volunteer advisory capacity before the university realized the need for professional staff and created either a part-time or a full-time position.[11] As I have seen through my own work, given the many needs that Muslim chaplain roles encompass for both the Muslim community and the whole university community, a volunteer or part-time position is often very demanding, and due to the

---

5. Omer Bajwa, interview with author, November 24, 2020.
6. Omer Bajwa, interview with author, November 24, 2020.
7. Omer Bajwa, interview with author, November 24, 2020.
8. Omer Bajwa, interview with author, November 24, 2020.
9. Omer Bajwa, interview with author, November 24, 2020.
10. Brown University, "Rumee Ahmed Appointed."
11. Omer Bajwa, interview with author, November 24, 2020.

sensitive nature of these positions and the issues they address, the opportunity to hire trained, experienced, and integrated professional staff is highly valuable to institutions.

The path to the development of Muslim chaplain positions is also revelatory of dynamics both in the Muslim community and on campuses. In general, the need began to arise from a growing, active Muslim community forming on campus, and at first the community often sought or appointed a volunteer leader.[12] In time, the needs of the university for a staff colleague in this role and the desire for parity and equity with other religious traditions and chaplains necessitated the university allocating financial resources for a chaplain.[13]

Today there are essentially two models of university religious life departments at private higher education institutions—a lean model with a dean or director of religious life and many affiliated campus ministers, priests, and rabbis sent by organizations external to the university; or a more robust model with a dean or director and several staff chaplains of major faith traditions who are hired directly by the university. In the case of Islam, as with Hinduism, Buddhism, and Humanism, there are not external national organizations to "send" campus ministers or staff to campuses for these traditions. Therefore, if universities and colleges desire to have expert professional staff for such positions, they must allocate institutional resources and hire chaplains to build these programs. While this requires an investment of resources, universities hiring their own chaplains has many benefits in terms of the ability to select well qualified candidates who support the university mission, who are accountable to its policies, who are available to serve the full institution, who are integrated into many units of the university, and who can serve many different needs such as working with prospective students, families, alumni, the local community, etc.

All of the Muslim chaplains I interviewed credited the important role of university administrators, and especially university chaplains or deans of religious life, in establishing the most robust Muslim chaplain roles.[14][15][16] In addition to securing administrative support and funding for these positions, an interesting consideration was the way in which the university

---

12. Omer Bajwa, interview with author, November 24, 2020.
13. Omer Bajwa, interview with author, November 24, 2020.
14. Omer Bajwa, interview with author, November 24, 2020.
15. Nisa Muhammad, interview with author, November 11, 2020.
16. Celene Ibrahim, interview with author, November 23, 2020.

chaplains framed or made sense of the establishment of the Muslim Chaplin role initially. In the case of Howard University, a prominent historically Black university in Washington, D.C. with a storied Christian chapel, the dean of the chapel who established the Muslim chaplain position connected it back to the interfaith vision of The Rev. Dr. Howard Thurman, the celebrated theologian, educator, and civil rights leader who was the first dean of Howard's Andrew Rankin Memorial Chapel.[17] As the current Howard Muslim chaplain, Dr. Nisa Muhammad said,

> My dean, Dean Bernard Richardson, in 1994, appointed the first Muslim chaplain at the university ... And when I was interviewing, I said, "Why would you do that? That's so totally against what anybody would have thought in 1994." But he said he was just following the tradition of Howard Thurman. So, Dr. Howard Thurman was the first dean of the chapel at Howard. And, he said, he was all about interfaith, he started the first interfaith church. ... He said, "That was the tradition that I knew, to serve people and to serve students. And so, I was just following that tradition. We had all these Muslim students, they didn't have anybody, I couldn't provide the pastoral care they needed, they needed a Muslim chaplain."[18]

Other universities that established their Muslim chaplain positions after September 11, 2001 were influenced both by the growing numbers of Muslim students on campus and by the need to address and reduce stereotypes. Several of the chaplains I interviewed cited Yale university chaplain Sharon Kugler's concept of "hospitality" being central to the vision of religious life at Yale that led to the establishment of both Muslim and Hindu chaplain positions.[19,20] In the case of Tufts University, where Dr. Celene Ibrahim served as Muslim chaplain, the institutional identity of Tufts as a historically Universalist institution was receptive to the idea of welcoming all religions in an inclusive manner. With its focus on peacemaking and civic engagement (Tufts established the first graduate school of international relations in 1933 and developed a unique College for Civic Life that traces its roots to 1954), the establishment of a Muslim chaplain position was natural both for serving a diverse student body and for furthering peace and

---

17. Nisa Muhammad, interview with author, November 11, 2020.
18. Nisa Muhammad, interview with author, November 11, 2020.
19. Omer Bajwa, interview with author, November 24, 2020.
20. Asha Shipman, interview with author, November 14, 2020.

civic education. As is known in the field, Tufts has been remarkable with its Muslim chaplain position by appointing three women to serve as Muslim chaplains consecutively—Shareda Hosein, Naila Baloch, and Celene Ibrahim—and thereby building a significant history of women's leadership in Muslim chaplaincy.[21]

Preparation

As positions are established and institutions search for Muslim chaplains, an obvious consideration is the kind of background and skills that are most important for Muslim chaplains, and the chaplains I interviewed shared a general consensus on three main criteria that are most important: a strong background in the Islamic sciences and Islamic studies, with a sensitivity to the diversity of the tradition; a background in the skills of chaplaincy, and especially in pastoral care through coursework and/or supervised experience; and familiarity with U.S. higher education. On the topic of Islamic education, Bajwa explained, "you have to have a working familiarity with the Qur'an, with Qur'anic studies, with Hadith literature, with what you would expect any sort of competent commentator in the public sphere on Islam to have so that they know what they're talking about."[22] Celene Ibrahim added, "if you're going to serve people from a variety of Muslim backgrounds, you really have to have experience in different kinds of Muslim communities. . . . You at least have to know where to point them, or the framework of what they're talking about, even if you don't necessarily know the exact rules that they're inquiring about."[23] Nisa Muhammad agreed, saying:

> you definitely have . . . to have a good understanding and grounding in the faith. You have to know the faith from a variety of different perspectives because Islam is not a monolith, so to speak. People come to Islam, this journey of Islam, from a variety of different perspectives. Like I said, I'm a convert. And so, there are people that were born Muslims, there are people that were born Muslims in other countries, born Muslims who speak different languages, born Muslims from different cultures as opposed to different countries. And so, to be able to have an understanding

---

21. Celene Ibrahim, interview with author, November 23, 2020.
22. Omer Bajwa, interview with author, November 24, 2020.
23. Celene Ibrahim, interview with author, November 23, 2020.

of all of that, you're not going to understand all of it, but be open enough and sensitive enough to understand what's going on.[24]

This leads to the second requirement, which each of the chaplains stressed, which was the importance of a background in chaplaincy skills and especially in pastoral care. Bajwa shared, "You really need to have, especially, I would say . . . to be trained as a chaplain . . . You need to have some serious pastoral training, whether it's CPE or classes in pastoral care and counseling. You can take an M.Div. in school or a seminary. I think that's totally a requisite."[25] Nisa Muhammad emphasized, "I think just being open and understanding of what young people go through, I think that's the other thing and especially understanding the vulnerability of young people, especially when it comes to faith."[26] Two of the chaplains I spoke with attended Hartford Seminary (Bajwa and Muhammad), and one attended Harvard Divinity School (Ibrahim) for chaplaincy and divinity studies. Along these lines, Nisa Muhammad mentioned a connection with the professional Association of Muslim Chaplains, as a resource for addressing issues that arise in chaplaincies, that has been helpful: "They have workshops, they have conferences, they have a specific group for university chaplains that meets twice a month now. But you can ask questions, what about this? What about this?"[27]

A third element important for Muslim chaplains, especially in the higher education setting, is familiarity with the higher education context and current intellectual and academic concerns. As Celene Ibrahim said, "If you want to work in a university setting, you really have to understand higher ed. Like my question is, can you just have a foundation in spiritual care and then understand higher ed on the job, or what do you have to understand about the higher ed space before coming in?"[28] Omer Bajwa seemed to feel, especially in the Yale environment, that a background in American higher education and the kinds of subjects and questions students are wrestling with, is very important:[29]

---

24. Nisa Muhammad, interview with author, November 11, 2020.
25. Omer Bajwa, interview with author, November 24, 2020.
26. Nisa Muhammad, interview with author, November 11, 2020.
27. Nisa Muhammad, interview with author, November 11, 2020.
28. Celene Ibrahim, interview with author, November 23, 2020.
29. Omer Bajwa, interview with author, November 24, 2020.

I think it really helps in my opinion, if someone has a strong background in the humanities or social sciences. Because I think so many of the conversations we're having with our communities, . . . as well as with the broader campus community, are really grounded in the social sciences. We're talking about critical race theory. We're talking about postcolonialism. We're talking about all of these. These are the intellectual currents that we're a part of. And so, our students are going to ask us questions about this.[30]

Given the fact that chaplaincy is not a traditional path for spiritual leadership in Islam, it may be that some of those who serve in Muslim chaplain positions, especially at the volunteer or part-time level, may not have all of these elements in their background. Ibrahim also mentioned other skills, such as nonprofit organizational management, being helpful, especially to lead larger, more developed programs.[31] Ideally, some combination of these three main elements is optimal for full-time positions.

Responsibilities

Each of the Muslim chaplains I interviewed indicated that their duties and responsibilities, and the shape of the programs they led or lead as Muslim chaplains, were slightly different and developed over time in relationship to the needs of the campuses they were serving. Nisa Muhammad's title, for instance, is actually "assistant dean of religious life," and in addition to offering Muslim chaplaincy, she serves a variety of communities at Howard, including arranging Passover seders, support for Hindu students, and programs for the students she calls, "the wanderers and the wonderers."[32] As an assistant dean, she also serves in the office and offers pastoral care and counseling to students of all religions and backgrounds.[33] When she first came to Howard, she describes that the Muslim life program consisted of Jumu'ah prayers that took place in a men's residence hall, and other events that capitalized on Howard's high profile as a university and part of the Washington, D.C. community.[34] However, she found that not all students were being served, and she decided to place an emphasis on all students,

---

30. Omer Bajwa, interview with author, November 24, 2020.
31. Celene Ibrahim, interview with author, November 23, 2020.
32. Nisa Muhammad, interview with author, November 11, 2020.
33. Nisa Muhammad, interview with author, November 11, 2020.
34. Nisa Muhammad, interview with author, November 11, 2020.

and accessibility to the whole student community.[35] Jumu'ah prayers were moved to a more neutral and less gendered space, and a variety of different imams and leaders were invited to lead in order to allow students to benefit from leaders of multiple backgrounds and perspectives.[36] In addition, Muhammad has placed emphasis on programming that has addressed the particular needs of her students. To address issues about skin color and beauty in Islam, which has not always valued Black beauty, for instance, she adopted a program called "Hijabfest," that invited Muslim supermodels to come to campus and speak about beauty and fashion.[37] Also, recognizing that Muslim students are often in the minority at HBCUs, and that Black Muslim students are often a minority on other campuses, she and her students began to host Black Muslim student conferences to allow students to experience and explore a larger community.[38]

In describing the Muslim chaplaincy program at Tufts, Celene Ibrahim shared that her predecessors had already worked to transition the Tufts program from a more male-dominated environment and not as much of a community as a place to pray the Friday prayers, to being a multi-gender and multi-ethnic spiritual community, inclusive of Muslims of many backgrounds.[39] The leadership of the Muslim Students Association was also strong—a group that Ibrahim advised and worked with, along with a Muslim Cultural House and Islamic societies at several of Tufts' graduate and professional schools.[40] Also, Ibrahim emphasized a focus on building intra-Muslim relations and also interfaith relations, helping the Muslim community to become a partner with other groups on campus, whether religious and philosophical, or identity related, or connected with social justice and civic life. Examples were programs such as Eid celebrations on the main university green, that allowed for greater visibility for the holiday and an easy way for newcomers to get involved, and workshops on being Muslim in politics and activism.[41] Ibrahim said,

> I was just also thinking a lot about civic activism, and the ways in which a community based at a university could be involved in

---

35. Nisa Muhammad, interview with author, November 11, 2020.
36. Nisa Muhammad, interview with author, November 11, 2020.
37. Nisa Muhammad, interview with author, November 11, 2020.
38. Nisa Muhammad, interview with author, November 11, 2020.
39. Celene Ibrahim, interview with author, November 23, 2020.
40. Celene Ibrahim, interview with author, November 23, 2020.
41. Celene Ibrahim, interview with author, November 23, 2020.

intellectual questions of justice . . . The university provides this great platform for thinking about either religion and race, religion and poverty . . . And so just having this really large campus with a lot of professional schools—it's a great opportunity for not only meeting Muslim students with their spiritual care needs, but thinking about questions about religion and society more broadly, as well.[42]

Ibrahim was interested in helping young Muslims understand that how they pray and how they fast should be connected with their ethical commitments and their civic life and professional life as community leaders—helping the community transition from being a minority community "on the down low," to being visible and engaged.[43] Since 9/11, she says, there was not the choice to be unseen, and so the question became how to be seen.[44] This also connected with a sense of responsibility not to let non-Muslim students graduate without any knowledge of Islam or with stereotypes of Islam, a "cultural diplomacy piece." In her vision, what universities like Tufts should offer is not merely training for a profession but training for civic leadership.[45]

Speaking about his program at Yale, Omer Bajwa echoed and emphasized many of these themes, especially the idea of the Muslim community as a place for social and moral development.[46] In order to cultivate deeper intersectional community and break down silos of age, culture, race, nationality, ethnicity, language, sect, degree program, and even status as a campus or community member, Bajwa developed a tradition of Friday dinners in Yale's Battell Chapel during Ramadan where all would be invited to be together for potluck as a diverse and open community. Bajwa provided the basis for dinner and then said, "You can make it potluck style. If you want to, cook additional biriani and bring it. You want to cook baklava, whatever it is. Let's make this fun. And so, we would get like 200 people, 250 people, people would be bringing their professors, their advisors, their suitemates, their roommates, And so it's just a big party . . . Every Friday night we do that in Battell." Part of his purpose, he explains, is also to help Muslim students bridge to life after university, where they may not have as

---

42. Celene Ibrahim, interview with author, November 23, 2020.
43. Celene Ibrahim, interview with author, November 23, 2020.
44. Celene Ibrahim, interview with author, November 23, 2020.
45. Celene Ibrahim, interview with author, November 23, 2020.
46. Omer Bajwa, interview with author, November 24, 2020.

ready-made a Muslim community and circle of friends, but they can learn how to build one.[47]

Bajwa describes his overall program as having five main parts, which are listed on his website: religious programming, spiritual care and mentoring, interfaith engagement, educational outreach and teaching, and student advising and advocacy.[48] He spoke of his starting into chaplaincy in large measure through interfaith work, speaking on behalf of Muslim associations about Islam and Muslims after 9/11. But a clear passion of his is education, and especially education and formation for moral leadership. On a personal level, this involves the question, "What does it mean to adult in today's world and to try to have integrity and try to live by certain values and ethics?" and on a social level it is a question of leadership,[49]

> What I found is a lot of our students are really thirsting for, what does it mean to be a leader? . . . [Our universities] produce leaders in science, technology, the humanities, intellectual frontiers. . . . I want Islam to be a voice in the conversation. Of course, I want you to read like James Baldwin and Ibram X. Kendi, *How to Be an Antiracist,* and read queer theories, read all of that . . . And where as a Muslim do you find spiritual value or a spiritual voice in that conversation? ... So we take that on, not in a formal way, but in my sermons, in my one-on-ones with students, in the kind of programming we do, the kind of conversations we want to have.[50]

Challenges

Chaplain Omer Bajwa speaks of the rigorous and critical academic environments of elite higher education institutions in the United States as one of the challenges in a way to Muslim chaplaincy and spiritual life programs. Even in his own journey, there was a tension between being able to pursue rigorous academic study, such as that leading to a Ph.D., and remain involved and in leadership in the Muslim community.[51] The demands of academic life can make maintaining a spiritual life challenging. In addition, as Bajwa described, it is sometimes a challenge to bring academic discourses into

---

47. Omer Bajwa, interview with author, November 24, 2020.
48. Yale University, "Muslim Life at Yale."
49. Omer Bajwa, interview with author, November 24, 2020.
50. Omer Bajwa, interview with author, November 24, 2020.
51. Omer Bajwa, interview with author, November 24, 2020.

conversation with Islam.[52] In some cases even institutionally, occasionally philosophies and cultural needs can come into conflict, such as the Muslim cultural value of modesty and the contemporary liberal university value of deconstructing gender differences by instituting all-gender residence hall floors and even shared bathrooms as a way of deconstructing gender differences.[53] At many institutions, the housing lottery time has become a challenge, especially for Muslim students who view sharing residential floors and bathrooms with another gender to conflict with their cultural practices and expectations.[54] Each year, Bajwa said, chaplains advocate for more a culturally-sensitive approach and accommodation for the needs of these students.[55] He said,

> It becomes a privacy issue, it becomes an issue of comfort, it becomes an issue of modesty, of saying if it was all women . . . I could walk to the shower in my bathrobe and not have to have hijab on, to be dressed. But if I know that there's like five guys in the suite next door or down the hall, and we're all sharing the same bathroom, there's just this constant level of being on alert.[56]

This raises the question of how universities should balance some students' cultural value of modesty in relationship with liberal perspectives on gender. To some degree, this is a challenge for the chaplain as an administrator as well, because the chaplain is charged with both advocating for religious accommodations as well as supporting institutional policies.[57]

Another challenge cited by the interviewees had to do with the question of the chaplain's own identities, or the impossibility of one person being the chaplain for an entire and remarkably diverse community. On various campuses across the country doing searches for Muslim chaplains, there have been questions about the identities of the chaplains—whether around the candidate's gender, or identity as a convert or someone raised in the faith from birth, or around ethnic background, etc. Additionally, there have been questions whether traditional Islamic education is essential, or a Western Islamic studies education is sufficient, along with the place of Shi'a and Isma'ili identities in predominantly Sunni communities, for instance.

52. Omer Bajwa, interview with author, November 24, 2020.
53. Omer Bajwa, interview with author, November 24, 2020.
54. Omer Bajwa, interview with author, November 24, 2020.
55. Omer Bajwa, interview with author, November 24, 2020.
56. Omer Bajwa, interview with author, November 24, 2020.
57. Omer Bajwa, interview with author, November 24, 2020.

All of these are complexities that institutions and chaplains must manage in their particular contexts. And they bring into tension core Islamic beliefs and teachings about essential common human dignity and the very real historical and cultural dimensions of gender, race, ethnicity and other differences. These issues can even raise the question of whether more than one person is needed to serve as a chaplain for a large program. Bajwa shared that his wife also acts as an informal chaplain to parts of the community, and in other settings too, spouses and assistant chaplains have brought different identities into the program.[58]

Several of the chaplains mentioned that there was a time, in the earlier days of Muslim chaplaincy, when the role of a Muslim chaplain was not well understood in higher education settings. Some Muslims had questioned the use of the term "chaplain" since it derives from Christian tradition and is not necessarily indigenous to Islam. But most said that students entering universities today are often more aware and accepting of the role of Muslim chaplains.[59] For those who have questions, chaplains like Nisa Muhammad focus on pastoral care, another Christian-rooted term, but a practice found in analogous ways in Islam. She says, "The thing is, you have to help people understand how Prophet Muhammad, peace and blessings be upon him, did pastoral care. That he was in fact a chaplain to his community. And so, put it in terms that people can understand."[60] All of the chaplains mentioned Dr. Ingrid Mattson, the founder of the Muslim Chaplaincy program at Hartford Seminary, as an early example of a Muslim chaplain and a woman in chaplaincy leadership. According to Celene Ibrahim, "She . . . helped formalize this idea that there is a professional route to Muslim leadership that did not look like going to Al-Azhar, or going to Qom, or going to one of these ancient, medieval . . . established centers of Islamic learning" as the only pathway.[61]

The fact that there is not an established tradition of Muslim chaplaincy, despite the many useful roles it plays in U.S. higher education contexts, means that there is no national "sending body" or support body backing Muslim chaplains, as developed in the Catholic community through Newman Centers and the Jewish community through organizations like Hillel and Chabad. Celene Ibrahim spoke of looking to the Hillel Jewish

---

58. Omer Bajwa, interview with author, November 24, 2020.
59. Celene Ibrahim, interview with author, November 23, 2020.
60. Nisa Muhammad, interview with author, November 11, 2020.
61. Celene Ibrahim, interview with author, November 23, 2020.

community at Tufts as an example of how to develop a thriving religious life program, although there is no equivalent national network like Hillel for Muslims, and Ibrahim says that Muslims may be unlikely to develop that, given Muslim preferences for localized leadership.[62] While there is a national Muslim Students Association, she has not had extensive contact with it, and even the national association of Muslim chaplains she shared is a fairly small circle of the people in these roles:

> a professional association that's run very part time by people who are really stretched thin. If they wanted to grow it, . . . they would probably need to invest in staff to make it more sustainable. And in order to do that, you would need to charge higher dues, and in order for that, you'd need to have a professional base getting paid at a reasonable rate."[63]

So, while a national organization that would send Muslim chaplains to campuses might be helpful, especially for public institutions that are unlikely to hire Muslim chaplains for religion-state separation reasons, the likelihood of that in the short term seems small.

These types of sentiments connect with another challenge that virtually all the chaplains I interviewed raised, which was one of compensation. Chaplain Ibrahim said,

> I think just people, and not me personally, but the feeling is, of just wanting to be better compensated, so that the actual work could happen. Because people are in a place where they're doing what needs to be done out of their sense of commitment and their sense of passion and dedication. . . . But it's also like a profession. And I think some people feel that they're not recognized as professionals, as anyone else on the campus.[64]

This may be rooted in the American idea of religion and volunteerism. And yet, while some positions may be volunteer, or part time, or not well compensated, the student, faculty, and staff needs for chaplaincy support are real, and chaplains are responding. Chaplains often provide spiritual leadership, but for marginalized communities, chaplains also provide support more aligned with social work, helping people with practical needs such as

---

62. Celene Ibrahim, interview with author, November 23, 2020.
63. Celene Ibrahim, interview with author, November 23, 2020.
64. Celene Ibrahim, interview with author, November 23, 2020.

moving, finding housing, finding jobs, and finding clothing or a doctor in perhaps a new country or region.[65]

Other chaplains I interviewed spoke about the fact that part-time roles might not offer benefits like healthcare, which chaplains need for themselves and their families, and if they want to dedicate themselves to their work, it is very difficult to do that in a part-time way, to truly be present for students nights and weekends and when they are needed and wanted as part-time staff.[66] Similarly, some chaplain positions that are paid ten months a year, or do not include paid summers, do not allow for the kind of reflection and preparation necessary to do good educational work or the professional development that is crucial for remaining prepared to preach, teach, care, and serve.[67]

Beyond that, any kind of program development or institutional work—such as cultivating alumni and parent connections or planning and fundraising—is very difficult to accomplish in the throes of the academic year. And in Islam, important seasons and occasions like Ramadan and Eid may occur in the summer. As Ibrahim shared,

> It's just another plug for thinking about these positions as full time, yearlong. If you want a strong program, you have to have time for planning and visioning, and you're setting things in place. And especially when you have rotating holidays like you do with the Islamic calendar, it's helpful if you know that you're going to be employed when your students are celebrating their major holiday."[68]

In short, the goal would be for universities to regard chaplains as they would any other counselor, diversity director, or advisor—as professionals working full time, year-round.

Future

According to the Pew Research Center, Muslims are currently "the fastest growing religious group in the world."[69] Islam is the world's second largest

---

65. Celene Ibrahim, interview with author, November 23, 2020.
66. Omer Bajwa, interview with author, November 24, 2020.
67. Celene Ibrahim, interview with author, November 23, 2020.
68. Celene Ibrahim, interview with author, November 23, 2020.
69. Pew Research Center, "Muslims and Islam."

religion after Christianity, and if trends continue, Muslims will exceed the number of Christians by the end of this century.[70] In the United States, there are an estimated 3.45 million Muslims, or about 1.1% of the U.S. population, but numbers are growing: projections estimate that Muslims will comprise 2.1% of the U.S. population by 2050, exceeding people who identify as Jewish religiously, and becoming the second largest faith group in the country (not counting the nonreligious).[71] The Muslim American community is made up in large measure of immigrants from around the world, with three-quarters of U.S. Muslims being immigrants or the children of immigrants.[72] And the U.S. Muslim demographic has been swiftly increasing from a modest starting point by about 100,000 people per year, driven by increases due to birthrate and by immigration of Muslims to the U.S.[73] In light of this, colleges and universities should expect increasing rates of Muslim students each year, as the chaplains I interviewed noted that they are experiencing in their campus communities.

The chaplains I interviewed made several points about the growth of the Muslim community and what that should mean for the future of Muslim chaplaincy. This included the idea that a growing Muslim community has particular needs, and that if universities and colleges are serious about their diversity, equity, and inclusion goals, then supporting this underrepresented and growing community—and a community that faces social prejudice and stereotypes—is an important part of universities serving their diverse communities in the best possible ways. They also expressed that as the needs of Muslim students are met, it contributes to the university reaching its other outcomes, in terms of student academic success as well as personal wellbeing and ethical and leadership development.[74]

In addition, in a context of continued prejudice and stereotypes against Muslims, and the widespread illiteracy about Islam across the United States, having opportunities to reduce stereotypes and learn about Islam is crucial to advance universities' educational mission for all students, to be graduating global citizens and leaders. Muslim chaplaincies can contribute to the outcomes of academic success, student wellness, and moral and leadership development for all students, faculty, and staff. In light of that,

---

70. Pew Research Center, "Muslims and Islam."
71. Pew Research Center, "Muslims and Islam."
72. Pew Research Center, "Demographic Portrait of Muslim Americans."
73. Pew Research Center, "Demographic Portrait of Muslim Americans."
74. Celene Ibrahim, interview with author, November 23, 2020.

Muslim chaplaincy training programs are likely to continue to grow, with educational institutions taking on or exploring this area as an education pathway, and one that these Muslim chaplains see as important for other underrepresented traditions as well, including Hinduism and Buddhism.[75]

As Yale's Muslim chaplain Omer Bajwa shared,

> Where we're at now, where I think we're going to go, is the Muslim community is only growing . . . so, just raw data. Population-wise there's more and more Muslim kids that are applying to campuses . . . [And in addition,] we live in an age of increased racial and ethnic awareness, right? We talk about race, ethnicity, migration, . . . indigeneity. We talk about all these subjects on our campuses. So, what that means is I think there are allies and there's support for—how do we not just support our Black community and our Latinx community and an LGBTQ community on campus, but who are the other identity groups?[76]

Bajwa raises the interesting and important point that campus Muslim communities are not only a religious community, or a community of belief, but they are in fact a cultural community (albeit multicultural), and they could be viewed as such in the ways that campuses provide support for different cultural groups. He continued,

> "Do we look at Muslims as a cultural group? Do we look at them as a religious group? As a faith community? How do we support them better? And I think that is also the push, right? Against a sort of systemic negligence in the past that other people are saying, no, we need to do better. Let's do better. And let's help them out and do more for them. So, I think it's going to grow. The field of Muslim chaplaincy and the broader scope."[77]

Celene Ibrahim also raised this theme of the universities' need to support their growing Muslim communities as an issue of equity in their diversity, equity and inclusion goals and its connection to enhancing positive outcomes for students: "It's a commitment to serve students . . . all these institutions have diversity statements. And it's a moment to think about, are we actually doing what we say we're doing, what we aspire to be doing? So there's a certain amount of integrity that I think is involved."[78]

---

75. Nisa Muhammad, interview with author, November 11, 2020.
76. Omer Bajwa, interview with author, November 24, 2020.
77. Omer Bajwa, interview with author, November 24, 2020.
78. Celene Ibrahim, interview with author, November 23, 2020.

Meeting this underrepresented community's needs translates into greater academic satisfaction and success for the whole university community. Ibrahim continued, "I think if you're thinking outcomes, like student outcomes, if you're supporting students in their wellness, and recognizing that for a lot of people, spirituality is part of wellness, you're going to get better outcomes. . . . if people are well, they might not engage in risky behavior or self-harm."[79] Chaplain Nisa Muhammad agreed,

> I think for higher education people to look at the research that shows how important religious life is for university students, that religious life plays such a key role in a student's life in terms of improving their academics, increasing retention, all the variables by which religious life acts to secure a student's identity and understanding of who they are as a person of that university, the research is there . . . . But the research is not just there for Christian students, the research should also support Muslim students and students of other faith traditions as well. It's not even just the Muslim students. As they can, universities should also offer programming or services to students of other faith traditions as well. Because the research shows that religious life is critical, it's really important for a lot of students . . .[80]

Ibrahim spoke of this as part of a "holistic education" that is available for the whole community:

> Muslim chaplains who are in the higher ed space, really are resources for the whole community, and it can be set up like that. And that's one of the things I think we did really well at Tufts, that we made possible, is to be chaplains for the entire university. And I think if institutions are just thinking about Muslim chaplaincy and just thinking about their Muslim students, they're missing a lot. So, I think it's that more holistic education, the opportunities that someone with these specializations and with these networks and connections can open up, is really important.[81]

Muslim chaplaincy simultaneously serves the twin needs of supporting an underrepresented community while also addressing, educating, and serving a larger non-Muslim majority community to reduce stereotypes and be educated holistically. This might be specifically related to prejudice

---

79. Celene Ibrahim, interview with author, November 23, 2020.
80. Nisa Muhammad, interview with author, November 11, 2020.
81. Nisa Muhammad, interview with author, November 11, 2020.

and stereotype reduction, but also to moral and leadership development. As Nisa Muhammad says,

> A lot of people don't understand or know about Islam, and I want the students that I work with to be a good example of that in whatever way they can. I want them to be ethical students, and I want them to understand the values and morals that Islam is supposed to engrain in them as young people. You're in the process of changing your mind. I mean, you're only going to be on this campus for four years. What kind of footprint are you going to leave? What kind of imprint do you want to take away? How do you want your experiences here to be with you forever?[82]

In the minds of the Muslim chaplains I interviewed, moral education and development for the Muslim community, prejudice and stereotype reduction, and education and leadership development for all students are interrelated. As Nisa Muhammad shared, "I want to be able to cultivate myself primarily. And then with the students that I work with, the ability to be a good leader, to be faithful, to have the ability to express your love for God in a variety of different ways. I want students to be able to show, to be able to smash stereotypes about Islam."[83] Nisa Muhammad speaks eloquently about the moral and leadership purpose of education for all students:

> Well, I think what's most important is, number one, understanding young people are in the process of changing their minds. I mean, that's number one. Some come with set ideas and set understandings about a thing, but they really want to know more, they really want to do better and they really want to be in an environment that allows them to develop leadership skills, ethical skills, and moral values that help them to be better citizens in the world. And I think that is one of the things that's very important that I kind of learned over time, that they don't come to college, 'I just want to be A, B, C and D, I just want to get a degree in business administration and go out and be an accountant.' They want so much more from a university experience.[84]

For Muslim students, she suggests, their ethical development is connected to "smashing stereotypes": "the media puts such a terrible spin on Islam. I mean, everybody's a terrorist or whatever. And so it's just, be an

---

82. Nisa Muhammad, interview with author, November 11, 2020.
83. Nisa Muhammad, interview with author, November 11, 2020.
84. Nisa Muhammad, interview with author, November 11, 2020.

ambassador. And I tell the students, I said, 'The closest somebody gets to reading the Qur'an is you.' You may be as close as they get to understanding Islam, to reading the Qur'an, so what did they learn about it from you?"[85]

Finally, Bajwa and other Muslim chaplains echoed that the future growth of the Muslim community and of Muslim chaplaincy should also parallel that of other communities. As Bajwa said, "I think you rightfully framed it in terms of multifaith chaplaincy is going to grow, because now more and more places are hiring Buddhist chaplains and Hindu chaplains for their underrepresented communities."[86] Nisa Muhammad said of Muslim chaplaincy, "I mean, it's a growing field, it's absolutely a growing field because Muslims are everywhere. So, there are Muslim sports chaplains or hospital chaplains, prison chaplains, university chaplains. It's a growing field because Muslims are found everywhere."[87] She continued:

> I think there'll be more schools, more accredited schools offering programs in Muslim chaplaincy. Right now, there are only a few that do that. And so, I think more schools will see the value and need for that. ... So, I think just getting people to see the value of incorporating, even if it is just to do interfaith, . . . just to see the need of expanding people's world viewpoint about faith traditions, because it's a big world and people are coming across so many people from so many different traditions. And if you're just blind to it, you're really going to be lost and you're going to be left behind.[88]

---

85. Nisa Muhammad, interview with author, November 11, 2020.
86. Omer Bajwa, interview with author, November 24, 2020.
87. Nisa Muhammad, interview with author, November 11, 2020.
88. Nisa Muhammad, interview with author, November 11, 2020.

2

Hindu Chaplaincy

History

THE HISTORY OF HINDU chaplaincy at universities and colleges in the United States is more recent than that of Muslim chaplaincy. At a number of campuses such as Harvard and MIT, for some decades, local swamis from urban Vedanta Societies have served as voluntary chaplains part time, available to speak at holiday celebrations and to offer pastoral care to students. According to the MIT website, Swami Tyagananda, who has been a monk of Swami Vivekananda's Ramakrishna order since 1976, has been head of the Vedanta Society of Boston and has served as a volunteer chaplain at Harvard and MIT.[1] The Boston Vedanta Society was established in 1909.[2] Swami Tyagananda advises MIT's Hindu Students Council and offers weekly meetings at the Vedanta Society that include prayer, guided meditation, the study of spiritual texts, and informal discussions.[3]

Swami Vivekananda's lecture at the Chicago Parliament of the World's Religions in 1893 was a watershed moment for the visibility, awareness, and expansion of Hinduism in America. Still, it was over a century later before Princeton University created the first paid Hindu chaplain position at a U.S. university in 2008, hiring Vineet Chander. (That position became full-time and permanent in 2009.) Also in 2008, the University of Southern California appointed Varun Soni to be dean of religious life—Soni is the first Hindu to serve as a dean of religious life in the U.S., and he has

---

1. MIT Spiritual Support, "Swami Tyagananda."
2. Ramakrishna Vedanta Society of Massachusetts, https://vedantasociety.net.
3. MIT Spiritual Support, "Swami Tyagananda."

appointed a number of part-time Hindu advisors at USC.[4] In 2013, Yale created a paid part-time Hindu chaplain position and hired Asha Shipman, and her position became full time in 2016.[5] In 2014, Georgetown appointed its first paid part-time Hindu chaplain, Pratima Dharm, who had served as the first Hindu chaplain in the U.S. military.[6] That role was expanded to full time in 2016 with the hire of Brahmachari Vrajvihari Sharan. And after requests by the Hindu Students Association and advocacy work we were able to do while serving as university chaplain at Tufts, Tufts hired its first paid part-time Hindu chaplain in the fall of 2020. Emory also hired its first full-time Hindu chaplain in December 2020, as part of Emory's new multifaith model for religious life. These are currently the main paid Hindu chaplain roles at U.S. universities. A number of other universities have had volunteer advisors or graduate student volunteers, such as Columbia and NYU. But the field of Hindu chaplaincy in American higher education is still quite young, with just four paid full-time positions (i.e., Princeton, Yale, Georgetown, and now Emory).

Since Hinduism has been in America since the early 1900s, and U.S. campuses have had a significant numbers of South Asian students since the children of the 1965 New Immigration from West, South, and East Asia began to arrive at U.S. universities in the 1990s and 2000s, one question might be why the development of Hindu chaplaincy at U.S. universities is still at such an early phase. One answer may be that institutions have been unaware of the growing number of their students who are Hindu or followers of other South Asian religions, as well as the fact that Hinduism in America has not been nationally organized in a way that would allow for the proactive and strategic establishment of campus ministries, as the Roman Catholic Church did with Newman clubs starting in 1893 and the Jewish community did with Hillel foundations starting in 1923.

Vineet Chander, the first paid full-time Hindu chaplain at U.S. university, described how, as an undergraduate at Carnegie Mellon University, it would not have occurred to him to advocate for a Hindu chaplain position.[7] He was involved in the Hindu Students Association, but he said at that time, just to book space and celebrate a puja or holiday together was the students' idea of success:

4. University of Southern California, "Historic Appointment of Hindu as Dean."
5. Chaplaincy Innovation Lab, "Hindu Chaplaincy in U.S. Higher Education."
6. Georgetown University, "Former Army Chaplain."
7. Vineet Chander, interview with author, November 20, 2020.

> When I was an undergrad, if we got, forget dedicated space, if we were just able to book a room, we were very grateful and self-congratulatory. We were like, "Yes, we did it!" You know? "We booked a room, and we lit some candles, and celebrated Diwali." I sound a little snarky when I say that, but at that time that was considered, you just, at least, I won't speak for others, but for myself I had so deeply internalized, how could I even ask for anything else? What is there even more to ask for?[8]

Chander, who is the son of immigrants, attributes this outlook to the notion that institutions like American higher education were not set up to welcome and support the kind of diversity that a Hindu campus community would represent, and that somehow he felt it might be inappropriate or impertinent to expect it. He continued,

> I was actually raised in, maybe it might be a typical child of immigrant experience, but my parents, it was like, "You are there to study. Put your head down. Don't make waves." There was none of this, "Go out and advocate and represent." It was like, "Do what you got to do. You're not there to start revolutions and advocate for this or that. You get your stuff done. If you have some free time and you want to do this stuff, fine." It was almost like, "Okay, but don't let it interfere with your studies."[9]

This was even though support for other religious life was present on campus, and even though faith and spirituality were important to him. Chander continued, "coming from that background, it would not have even occurred to any of us to ask about. And I'm sure our Christian classmates had their chaplains and were doing their thing. And there were Hillel centers. We knew about this stuff. But there was such a cognitive dissonance where it was like, 'Yeah, well, of course. My Jewish friend goes to Shabbat at the Hillel and I may even go with them. But I would never [expect that].'"[10]

Chander's own journey included what has been a step toward the development of Hindu chaplaincy at a number of universities, which was his serving as a volunteer Hindu advisor while he was a graduate student at George Washington (GW) University Law School.[11] After college, Chander felt a desire to deepen his spirituality and go on a spiritual journey to India

---

8. Vineet Chander, interview with author, November 20, 2020.
9. Vineet Chander, interview with author, November 20, 2020.
10. Vineet Chander, interview with author, November 20, 2020.
11. Vineet Chander, interview with author, November 20, 2020.

Hindu Chaplaincy

where he studied at an ashram. When he returned to start law school, the Hindu Students Association at GW asked him if he would serve as a volunteer advisor for them. He agreed, and he enjoyed that experience, but he assumed that it could only be a volunteer opportunity. Later on, after practicing law for a few years, he was considering returning to graduate school for religion and was volunteering as a Hindu advisor at Rutgers, when the professional position at Princeton opened up.

One reason that the idea of "chaplaincy" per se has not been seen as an available professional path in the Hindu community is that "chaplaincy" is not a kind of spiritual leadership that is indigenous to Hinduism. Chander said, before being invited to serve as the volunteer graduate student advisor at GW, he had never heard the term "chaplain": "Maybe I knew it from reruns of M*A*S*H, where I just thought it was the priest in the context of wartime or in a hospital or something like that. But I learned that, no, there was a multifaith kind of chaplaincy team at GW."[12] Additionally, Chander speaks of September 11, 2001 as a turning point in his own understanding of chaplaincy, since before that his service as a graduate student advisor mostly meant being a facilitator of student programs, such as a Bhagavad Gita study group. But with 9/11, GW's chaplain and spiritual advisors were "activated into holding space and vigils and grief counseling."[13] Given GW's proximity to the ground zeros in DC and given the fact that the Hindu community included so many international students, 9/11 hit the community hard, and in the context of the tragedy and the aftermath and war that followed, Chander and the other spiritual advisors felt called upon to serve as voices of hope on campus as well as a moral compass as political and social justice activism emerged.[14]

At the time, Chander thought of chaplaincy as something that only GW's multifaith chaplain, who was a Christian minister, would do, but the experience planted a seed of what the idea of chaplaincy might be in the Hindu community[15]. Although his official title is "Coordinator of Hindu Life" at Princeton, Chander has always informally claimed the title of "Hindu chaplain," and sees his work standing in the tradition of university

---

12. Vineet Chander, interview with author, November 20, 2020.
13. Vineet Chander, interview with author, November 20, 2020.
14. Vineet Chander, interview with author, November 20, 2020.
15. Vineet Chander, interview with author, November 20, 2020.

chaplaincy that includes William Sloan Coffin (the well-known social justice activist and university chaplain of Yale University) and others.[16]

He believes the notion of chaplaincy can evolve and offers a valuable concept that can be occupied in new ways for new communities as the demographics of religion in American higher education change.[17] He especially finds the idea of "pastoral care" relatable, as Hinduism includes theological images of Krishna, the personification of God revered in Vaishnava traditions, serving as a cowherd.[18] The idea of compassionate caring for souls in a pastoral way resonates with Chander. He and other Hindu chaplains note the relationship of Krishna to Arjuna in the Gita as a type of chaplaincy, with a personified god offering spiritual support and counsel.[19][20]

Others serving in Hindu chaplaincy roles such as Asha Shipman at Yale and Brahmachari Sharan at Georgetown share a complex relationship with the notion of Hindu chaplaincy and use the term loosely along with other terminology. Shipman's position at Yale was initially called "Hindu Fellow," which, having just completed her Ph.D. in anthropology, she thought might be a postdoctoral position. She uses the term "Hindu chaplain" mostly outside of the Hindu community as a shorthand for her work among colleagues. She shared that inside the Hindu community, she has experienced some skepticism about the term "Hindu chaplain," since in religious literature "chaplains" were mostly spiritual advisors to royalty and because some people she has spoken to thought that it meant "chaplain to the Hindus," as in a Christian chaplain who would be seeking to convert Hindus to Christianity. Inside the Hindu community, she uses her official Yale title of "Director of Hindu Life," which she believes describes her position well within higher education as a layperson responsible for supporting Hindu spiritual life.[21]

Georgetown University's Hindu chaplain Brahmachari Sharan is a clergyperson, having been a Hindu priest, and now being a renunciant in the Vedantic forest monastic tradition. He points out that chaplaincy in the Christian tradition itself is an evolution of the priesthood with an emphasis on counseling and care. In Hinduism, the role of a priest, or a ritual expert,

16. Vineet Chander, interview with author, November 20, 2020.
17. Vineet Chander, interview with author, November 20, 2020.
18. Vineet Chander, interview with author, November 20, 2020.
19. Vineet Chander, interview with author, November 20, 2020.
20. Asha Shipman, interview with author, November 15, 2020.
21. Asha Shipman, interview with author, November 15, 2020.

is one role; and the role of a guru, or spiritual teacher, is another. Sharan served as a priest and found himself being drawn into pastoral care, and he also possessed a strong interest in studying philosophy, which led to his earning a Ph.D. He says Georgetown viewed him as a kind of "Jesuit in Hindu robes"—as a priest, monastic, scholar, and teacher, which led to his appointment there. As he has challenged the idea of "Hinduism" itself, as a colonially invented term for the many diverse indigenous religious practices of South Asia, and as someone who now seeks to serve not only Hindus on his campus but also Buddhists, Jains, and Sikhs, he has adopted the term "Director of Dharmic Life," which seeks to indicate his inclusive support for practitioners of multiple South Asian religious traditions. In time, he would like to see Georgetown have coordinators for each.[22]

Preparation

The newness of Hindu chaplaincy both within the tradition itself and in the United States higher education context means that there are not yet conventional pathways to Hindu chaplaincy positions or training programs. The Hindu chaplains I interviewed had academic backgrounds in law, anthropology, and Sanskrit studies. Two (Chander and Shipman) were first generation children of American immigrants and laypeople, and one (Sharan) was a monastic and an immigrant from the United Kingdom. This group of Hindu chaplains stressed that given the newness of the field, they would recommend flexibility and fluidity in terms of the required qualifications for Hindu chaplains, or at least for applicants for Hindu chaplain positions, who may be able to secure additional education or training while working in their positions, as is sometimes possible in higher education positions. All the chaplains suggested that different levels of training might be needed for different levels of positions. Hindu advisor and part-time chaplain positions tend to begin with more logistical and programmatic responsibilities, such as arranging programming for weekly devotionals, holiday celebrations like Diwali and Holi or events like Saraswati pujas, temple visits, movie nights, guest speakers, study groups, and other similar programs. For such positions, some personal and formal education in Hindu or South Asian studies, coupled with experience in event planning and leadership might be sufficient. But for full-time positions and those that involve spiritual or pastoral care, the chaplains I interviewed suggested that

---

22. Vrajvihari Sharan, interview with author, November 20, 2020.

supervised training in pastoral care, such as that acquired through Clinical Pastoral Education (CPE) programs is needed.[23][24][25]

Yale's Hindu chaplain Asha Shipman, who has a Ph.D. in anthropology, was among those who stressed that knowledge of American higher education contexts is very helpful, as well as a training in research. For religious traditions as ancient and vast as Hinduism, it is impossible for any single chaplain to be aware of all of the traditions and practices that members of the campus community might bring from their families, backgrounds, or interests. Along these lines, the ability of a Hindu chaplain to understand how to and to actually conduct research and know where to go for answers and resources is necessary. Shipman said, "I always tell people, I am not a monk; I don't have a degree in religion. However, I am a researcher . . . . So if I don't know, I'll go and find out, or find somebody else who does. That, to me, is more important, that you have a humility about what you do and do not know, and that you're connected."[26] To that end, Shipman and other Hindu chaplains formed a North American Hindu Chaplains Association (NAHCA) in 2020, in part to serve as a network for sharing resources grounded in professional wisdom.[27] Shipman said, "NAHCA is there to give people connections. This is the professional association that if you ask someone, 'Tell me about Durga Puja,' somebody is going to know. Versus if you go onto the internet, you will find all sorts of stuff. That's the whole thing. We're aiming to be very resource rich."[28] NAHCA held its first conference May 23-24, 2020, online due to the COVID19 pandemic.[29] Through events such as that and a regular newsletter, the organization's leaders and members plan to help connect those serving in Hindu chaplaincy roles and support their professional growth.

All the Hindu chaplains I interviewed suggested that academic preparation in American higher education, usually through the attainment of a master's or doctoral degree, or the equivalent, is likely necessary to effectively serve as a full-time Hindu chaplain, because of the facility it offers in navigating the institutions and also the ability to intersect and be in

---

23. Vineet Chander, interview with author, November 20, 2020.
24. Vrajvihari Sharan, interview with author, November 20, 2020.
25. Asha Shipman, interview with author, November 15, 2020.
26. Asha Shipman, interview with author, November 15, 2020.
27. North American Hindu Chaplains Association, https://www.hinduchaplains.org.
28. Asha Shipman, interview with author, November 15, 2020.
29. Convergence on Campus, "North American Hindu Chaplaincy Conference."

conversation with the many diverse fields of study within the university. At the current time, however, academic programs specifically in Hindu chaplaincy are quite limited. The Oxford Centre for Hindu Studies is developing an online program,[30] and the Graduate Theological Union and Harvard Divinity School have been considering offering programs, but there are few clear pathways. The few Hindu chaplains in paid professional roles today have been dedicating their time to developing the emerging field, through giving interviews, making presentations, writing articles, papers, chapters, and books, forming the NAHCA professional association and holding its first conference, and consulting with graduate schools and divinity schools about potential academic programs. While all the chaplains I interviewed said that they find this exciting, it is also a challenge to be essentially developing the field while also working in it.[31,32,33]

Responsibilities

In terms of responsibilities, all the chaplains I interviewed recognized the work that many volunteer Hindu advisors who might be graduate students or potentially faculty or staff members might be doing. As Asha Shipman says, in her studies of Hindu chaplaincy, "I saw it as an interim step . . . I felt like it was an interim step which allowed an institution to dip their toe in the waters of this kind of chaplaincy care."[34] Some of the things that she and the other Hindu chaplains I interviewed might do might fall into this first category of the work that a Hindu advisor might offer. As Brahmachari Sharan described, "Once a week we do non-theist meditations, which are on the Vedanta. Those are my regular offerings. The festivals, the big ones we do. Diwali has just finished. Along with that, lots of panels, lots of interfaith engagements, those kinds of things, as you might expect would take place at Georgetown."[35] Shipman described some of the Hindu Students Council (now Organization) programs when she first started at Yale:

---

30. Vineet Chander, interview with author, November 20, 2020.
31. Vineet Chander, interview with author, November 20, 2020.
32. Vrajvihari Sharan, interview with author, November 20, 2020.
33. Asha Shipman, interview with author, November 15, 2020.
34. Asha Shipman, interview with author, November 15, 2020.
35. Vrajvihari Sharan, interview with author, November 20, 2020.

> When I joined, they were doing Holi and Diwali. And they were doing some movie nights, and they'd had some guest speakers. They'd been interested in scripture study to some degree. And they had a weekly puja, which wasn't really what I would have called a puja. It was a worship service, but it was not very organized in a way that a worship service would normally be if it's part of an institution. They had mantras, they had songs.[36]

Chander also described leading and facilitating similar programming as a graduate student Hindu advisor at both George Washington and Rutgers.[37]

As initially a part-time professional staff member at Yale, however, Asha Shipman described how she was able to provide more integration with the work of the university chaplaincy and to support and deepen the existing programming:

> When I started, I was 20 hours and I was coming in on Sundays to meet with my Hindu students organization board, and to do any kind of catch-up stuff. And then on Wednesdays, I pulled a 12-hour day. And then I did stuff at home too. But Wednesdays . . . I had staff meeting at 9:30 a.m., and then I had an event usually at 7:00 p.m. with the Hindu Students Council [now Organization], until 10:00 p.m. And what that meant was, everything was really condensed into those two days.[38]

Some of that work also involved considerable mapping about the resources at Yale connected to Hinduism and South Asia, "I spent probably the first year trying to learn about all the different departments and communities at Yale that had any kind of interest in South Asia or Hinduism, or culture, or anything related to what I was doing."[39] Additionally, Shipman was able to begin to build on and deepen the programming, "When [the students] said they wanted to expand their formal worship services to include a puja for the popular holy day Ramanavami, then I structured that with them. We had a workshop on the framework for conducting such a service with my dad, who has written a whole bunch of booklets on how to conduct pujas to the various deities. And he then trained them specifically for a Ramanavami puja"[40]

36. Asha Shipman, interview with author, November 15, 2020.
37. Vineet Chander, interview with author, November 20, 2020.
38. Asha Shipman, interview with author, November 15, 2020.
39. Asha Shipman, interview with author, November 15, 2020.
40. Asha Shipman, interview with author, November 15, 2020; Asha Shipman, email with author, March 25, 2021.

Hindu Chaplaincy

As the program has developed at Yale, it has taken on somewhat different shape, which Shipman described in the following way:

> In 2013, we added I think two or three of these formal pujas. And then we just kept building. And the community responded, in that we figured out what the graduate students wanted. They wanted a real puja. And we figured out that the undergraduates really liked to do mehndi. And we figured out that we could partner with the MSA and do a lot of things that were very South Asian. So, the programming really blossomed. And that was for the undergraduates, and slowly getting the graduate students in.[41]

Shipman realized that beyond worship, students had a desire for other types of learning and discussion, to different degrees and depths based on the knowledge of the tradition that they came to university with, that could deepen and integrate their knowledge of Hinduism:

> In time, we have shifted away from having a weekly puja. Instead, we incorporated other programs ... mostly spiritual, but with a cultural element in some cases. And having more opportunities to talk about everyday life, and how Hinduism is contributing. Because to me, that's so important. The students come to Hinduism through their families. And some of them have no background, and some of them have a ton of background. More and more, because the mandirs, the temples, are doing more for their Hindu students. I never got what they got, ever. I never had it.[42]

Beyond the students—undergraduate and graduate—and the postdocs whom she realized seemed especially underserved and supported, Shipman has also begun to offer more programming to support faculty and staff, especially in the difficult time of the COVID19 pandemic:

> Much of the suffering I've noticed in the past year has been amongst faculty and staff, who are definitely hurting. . . . I retooled one major program this fall so it directly supported staff and faculty. I offered a yogic breathing course that had a scientific basis to it, taught by a Sivananda yogi . . . After the spring I'd heard a lot from staff who were really frightened and exhausted, and subject to as many long Zoom hours as everybody else, but not getting much recognition for how hard that is. So, this *pranayama* course

---

41. Asha Shipman, interview with author, November 15, 2020.
42. Asha Shipman, interview with author, November 15, 2020.

was positioned on Wednesdays at noon to be a pause in the middle of the week. And was very well received.[43]

Undergirding this holistic support for all sectors of the campus community, including students, faculty, and staff, is Yale university chaplain Sharon Kugler's notion of university chaplaincy as the practice of radical hospitality in the institution, a concept that is an important value in many religious and philosophical traditions. Shipman said this approach to the work resonates deeply with her as a Hindu, "because in Hinduism, to be a host is actually fulfilling some of your karmic requirement. It is really important to be a host. Charitable giving is very, very important. Spirituality is imbued in everything you do."[44] Indeed, some Hindu mantras say that guests should be treated like gods, and that offering such hospitality is a deep spiritual duty. Having become full time allows even more opportunity to be present and available and actually provide that deep hospitality to the Hindu community as well as to everyone. Shipman said, "I am a university chaplain. I serve anybody who ... walks in and I'm there, I'm there for them . . . . if we're hired by the university, then we're more broadly intersecting with the communities in these institutions. And I think that's more robust."[45] Just having the time to integrate, rather than "order samosas and book speakers," has been very significant:

> What it allowed me to do was ... to have a greater physical presence on campus [so] that I could actually bridge more, I could do more cosponsoring of programs, and I had more time to go to people's offices . . . Because I like to go to people's offices and have conversations with them because it develops a strong interpersonal connection and opens the door for joint programming. I actually was more productive. I was three times more productive because I was there, and my creativity level flourished. And the amount of programming we did with HSO expanded dramatically.[46]

A key aspect of this hospitality, and one that Hindu chaplains can provide that can be especially meaningful to Hindu and other South Asian students, is the guidance these chaplains provide about navigating life as a religious and ethnic minority on a college and university campus in the

---

43. Asha Shipman, interview with author, November 15, 2020.
44. Asha Shipman, interview with author, November 15, 2020.
45. Asha Shipman, interview with author, November 15, 2020.
46. Asha Shipman, interview with author, November 15, 2020; Asha Shipman, email with author, March 25, 2021.

Hindu Chaplaincy

U.S. today. It is about having someone familiar with your experience and supportive who can serve as a counselor and guide when many others may not understand. She says Hindu chaplaincy allows these students to see,

> "Oh, hey, look. There's a place where I can go and celebrate my spirituality. And there's a person who I can talk with about whatever happens to be on my mind, who will understand even if it's not a perfect fit, will understand my background and my culture. And I won't have to go through the hurdles of explaining this to a mental health professional. It can take three sessions to go through all that. Whereas I walk in the door, and the Hindu chaplain has an understanding and deep appreciation for all that stuff. . . . So, there is certainly a way to help people feel welcome and able to be themselves while doing the work of being a student.[47]

Shipman sees Hindu chaplaincy programming as essentially helping to provide students with a spiritual "toolbox" to help navigate their lives, whether related to studies, work, relationships, family, career, society, or current events.[48] She says of her students:

> They're encountering so many racial and cultural challenges to what Hinduism is or isn't. I then decided, okay. What I need to give the students is a toolbox for how to deal with these questions. And the programming really reflected it. I had a Dharmic Discussions program that I started, where I invited speakers to talk about a particular value through their particular lens in Hinduism. We did gratitude one year. And the next year, we did resilience and equanimity. And this year, we talked about politics and social activism.[49]

Through Dharmic Discussions, students have the opportunity to connect their spirituality and values with the issues they are facing, as students and as growing human beings, in the context of a supportive community. Students have shared that they value Hindu chaplains as allies who can "read between the lines," who they can talk to and who has a safe space for them.[50]

Several chaplains echoed this and suggested that Hindu chaplaincy can be a complementary resource to student mental health care, especially for a community such as the South Asian community, some of whom have

---

47. Asha Shipman, interview with author, November 15, 2020.
48. Asha Shipman, interview with author, November 15, 2020.
49. Asha Shipman, interview with author, November 15, 2020.
50. Asha Shipman, interview with author, November 15, 2020.

tended to be more skeptical of Western notions of mental health. In traditional Hindu communities, Shipman says:

> If you want some sort of advice, you're going to go to either the guru, or you're going to go to a family member. Even seeking psychological, emotional, mental help in India, among the Indians, it's only recent. Like, since maybe the 1990s where it's even been talked about. And it's gaining traction now, but even in this country, if I want to find a mental healthcare provider who's South Asian, it is hard.[51]

Given that particular context, Brahamachari Sharan says that this kind of chaplaincy and the kind of community care it provides, "helps the student morale. It helps students who are out there with issues that there are on campus. It relieves a little bit the pressures from the psychiatric services that are offered . . . If you're able to deal with the very general stuff, then the more acute stuff can be routed correctly." [52]

Indeed, Shipman sees this kind of community-based care, community building, as at the heart of her work.[53] Part of this work is confronting and challenging the lack of understanding, stereotypes, and discrimination Hindus and practitioners of other South Asian religions face in the U.S. Even when Brahmachari Sharan was appointed at Georgetown, conservative publications criticized the move based on tropes of Hinduism being "pagan," "polytheistic," and "idolatrous."[54] Additionally, there is also perhaps a more "cultured" contempt in academic contexts. Because of such prejudice and discrimination, Shipman says,

> Hindus tend to be very private about their religiosity. And so they'll go to the temple, they'll go to the mandir, the ashram. They'll do their prayers, they'll congregate. But they're not necessarily using that kind of affiliation professionally. And that's why my position feels tenuous in many ways. Because I am, unlike so many professionals in my institution, very publicly Hindu.[55]

---

51. Asha Shipman, interview with author, November 15, 2020.
52. Vrajvihari Sharan, interview with author, November 20, 2020.
53. Asha Shipman, interview with author, November 15, 2020.
54. Pelletier, "Georgetown Appoints Hindu Chaplain."
55. Asha Shipman, interview with author, November 15, 2020; Asha Shipman, email with author, March 25, 2021.

Hindu Chaplaincy

In a way, the presence of the Hindu chaplain herself has opened up the possibility of being Hindu more publicly on campus, especially for faculty and staff. Shipman said,

> I have a bunch of faculty from different places around campus that attend my programs. So, they're folks from the sciences, from religion, from public health, from the medical school, and the divinity school. And it just feels like there are so many Indian professors who are a little worried about affiliation with being Hindu. But that's true, I think, across the board in public life. And this isn't really public life, but in a way it is. I mean, to be public about your faith traditions seems to be a big ask on college campuses for non-Christians. I feel like that's a real issue for them . . . it's just something that everybody has to negotiate in their own comfort level.[56]

Larger festivals seem to provide an easier opportunity for faculty and staff to connect with the Hindu community, in part because these have become somewhat, as Shipman describes, pan-Asian and campus-wide celebrations.[57] In addition, her identity as a leader and a scholar at these events allows her to help make other connections within the community, for support and mentoring:

> For example, if I find an undergraduate who says, "You know, Dr. Shipman, or Asha, I'm looking to go into neuroscience." And I'll say, "Oh, so-and-so is on our board and is in this lab. Why don't you talk to him or her right now? We're just eating dinner. And you can find out about that experience." Because a lot of what I think of as chaplaincy is actually making those connections. . . . when I think about what I do, I'm forming communities. And it's really central. Community building is really central. And so you meet the community where they are. And we're at a university, and the students want to have these opportunities. And yes, they'll come for puja, but they also are concerned about, "What am I going to do for an internship?" And in talking with them about what's important to them, if I can help them make linkages, then I think that is part of my job.[58]

In the Princeton context, Vineet Chander spoke of his role as building community, but also facilitating the spiritual and moral foundations of his students as they engage in their educations. Like Shipman, he spoke of the

---

56. Asha Shipman, interview with author, November 15, 2020.
57. Asha Shipman, interview with author, November 15, 2020.
58. Asha Shipman, interview with author, November 15, 2020.

ways in which, for Hindu Americans, the support structures that exist for other communities do not exist. He said:

> I'm sure every community feels this way and is entitled to feel this way. For the Hindu-American experience, from the Hindu-American community, it's especially critical, because I think in so many other ways, our faith, our community doesn't operate with the structures so many other communities have in place.... Having a person to help guide, facilitate, foster, to be . . . this kind of mentor for emerging adults.[59]

He went on to say that, given the time at university is such a formative time in students' lives, everything they are engaged in, from the curricular to the cocurricular is such a significant part of their development: "In that context, especially in this special, sacred, almost sacrosanct time of life, of discovery, of self-discovery formation . . . I can't even articulate how valuable it is to have the right person there to be a mentor, a friend, a sibling, whatever sort of imagery or metaphor you want to use. That to me, is just incalculable."[60]

Challenges

As Hindu chaplaincies have become established at U.S. universities, they have also faced some challenges. A primary one, as Princeton's Vineet Chander stated, has been the challenge of being understood by students and families who might not be looking or have a sense of what this resource provides.[61] For international students and families, it may be that they are more familiar with non-U.S. models of higher education which do not offer the kinds of residential campus community life and resources that most U.S. universities provide and believe are integral to the college experience. Although Chander states that awareness of his presence and program have grown, they still may not be resources that are anticipated and immediately understood, especially by students from overseas.[62] Chander said,

> Where I feel there's a lot of dissonance and surprise is with international students . . . whose families live outside of the U.S. ...

---

59. Vineet Chander, interview with author, November 20, 2020.
60. Vineet Chander, interview with author, November 20, 2020.
61. Vineet Chander, interview with author, November 20, 2020.
62. Vineet Chander, interview with author, November 20, 2020.

whose sort of more formative experiences, particularly around higher ed were like in India or elsewhere, like Singapore . . . Their paradigm of higher ed is quite different than I think the American paradigm of higher ed. So not only are they not used to thinking about chaplains, but in a lot of cases, they're not sort of used to thinking about student life generally.[63]

For others, students and families that are more acculturated to the U.S. context, given that chaplaincy is new in Hinduism, they still may not have a context of what a Hindu chaplain might be or do. One of Chander's early attempts to offer support and borrow best practices from his colleagues of other faiths was to offer office hours.[64] He noticed students streaming into his Christian colleagues' offices to check in and meet with them at certain times, and so he set up office hours, but at first no students came. He then asked a student leader of his, who explained that the practice to visit a chaplain's office hours would not be on Hindu students' radars, thus encouraging him to start inviting students out to coffee, which was more accessible, and they readily accepted.[65] Chander said:

> I discovered ... that students, particularly Hindu students who may not have a reference point, or who may be concerned about seeming weird by needing to talk to a chaplain, they may be scared away to come into my office and to do office hours. But if I say like, 'Hey, we should grab a cup of coffee, my treat.' They'll do that. .. And then .. that actually gave rise to .. students saying, 'Hey, do you have regular office hours? .. it doesn't always have to be over coffee. I can just come to your office.' And so, we ended up arriving there anyway, but it was almost like I had to take this route of, what felt right to them, what felt organic? I think a challenge, it continues to be a challenge, is just people within my community just don't have, they don't have a conceptual framework for this.[66]

This lack of a history of Hindu chaplaincy and a reference point, for students, alumni, and families, can also translate into a challenge of resources in terms of parent, alumni, and donor contributions that would support the program, or resources that would help the community. Despite the great success of the Hindu community in building large and beautiful

---

63. Vineet Chander, interview with author, November 20, 2020.
64. Vineet Chander, interview with author, November 20, 2020.
65. Vineet Chander, interview with author, November 20, 2020.
66. Vineet Chander, interview with author, November 20, 2020.

South Asian-style Hindu temples in many cities in the U.S., support for endowing chaplain positions at universities, which would help to keep a connection between university students and their faith, has not been as forthcoming. Securing support for staff or even for sacred spaces on campus, has largely not come from alumni, families, and donors if this is not in their philanthropic awareness. Brahmachari Sharan, who has been working to establish the Dharmic Life program at Georgetown and to open a campus sacred space for these communities (called a Dharmalaya), believes that a successful fundraising tactic from some initiatives in the South Asian community has been a minoritizing one—saying: "'We're a minority . . . We need to huddle. We need to save ourselves,' that kind of stuff. I don't do that," he said.[67] Brahamachari prefers to focus on the positive contributions and the potential that the Dharmic Life program and the Dharmalaya will have for the campus community. This is something that more recent alumni who have experience on campus are more likely to understand.[68] He also says, "So it has been the recent alumni of, say, the past ten years or so that have gone through university, have seen a place like Georgetown, and realize what the benefits would be because they've seen how, say, the Catholic community has benefited from the amount of investment [they have had]... or the Muslim community, or Jewish, etc."[69]

Another area that has been a challenge for some of the chaplains I interviewed has been building strong connection with the academic and curricular sectors of the university. On the one hand, at Georgetown, Brahmachari Sharan serves as an adjunct professor and teaches courses such as "Religions in Modern South Asia" and a course on "Religions without God."[70] Asha Shipman at Yale shared that while over time she is increasingly collaborating with Yale Divinity School and often partners with the Asian American Cultural Center, she shared that finding pathways to work with other units has sometimes been more challenging.[71]

At Princeton, when Vineet Chander arrived, his students shared that there was no professor on campus focused on Hinduism in the department of religion and that they desired more opportunities to learn about

---

67. Vrajvihari Sharan, interview with author, November 20, 2020.
68. Vrajvihari Sharan, interview with author, November 20, 2020.
69. Vrajvihari Sharan, interview with author, November 20, 2020.
70. Vrajvihari Sharan, interview with author, November 20, 2020.
71. Asha Shipman, interview with author, November 15, 2020; Asha Shipman, email with author, March 25, 2021.

Hinduism in a formal way.⁷² At first, he reached out to the department of religion, but he learned that there had been a longtime policy that the department did not co-sponsor programs with the office of religious life and the chapel. Chander believed this had been based on the notion that those in the office of religious life might not be purely objective and might even be anti-intellectual. Therefore, to address the challenge of the lack of opportunities to learn about Hinduism, Chander began to invite prominent national scholars of Hinduism to campus, such as John Hawley.

In time, the department began to relax its past approach and has even begun invite chaplains like Chander serve as respondents at academic lectures. This may also have to do with theoretical and methodological shifts in religious studies that have questioned notions of pure objectivity and sought to reconnect the study of religion with practices of "lived religion." In any case, while not every program offered on Hinduism by an academic department would be co-sponsored by the Hindu community and vice versa, there is an area of overlap in which speakers and programs that might be part of religious life can be seen as valuable to the study of religion, and those in the study of religion can be seen as potentially enhancing or enriching to religious life.⁷³

A fourth issue that those I interviewed shared has been a challenge to Hindu communities on campus has been ethical issues such as cultural appropriation and colonialism. According to the chaplain interviewees, there is an ongoing conversation in many Hindu communities on campus about the ways in which holiday celebrations like Holi or practices like yoga are offered through the Hindu community or not. Asha Shipman shared: "I went to the AAR and I sat in on a panel where the presenter was like, 'Yeah, [yoga] really doesn't have anything to do with Hinduism.' I was like, okay. I need to talk right now about how it does."⁷⁴ Brahmachari spoke of a similar dynamic about meditation, where it has been seen as fair game for appropriation by others. He said:

> One thing that came out in an *America* magazine that actually made me put pen to paper, and I've never done that before . . . They had a Jesuit who went to 'Ignatian Yoga' . . . and his report . . . was, 'It is delightful to see that no longer are . . . the fallen twisting and contorting themselves on the altars of false pagan gods but are

---

72. Vineet Chander, interview with author, November 20, 2020.
73. Vineet Chander, interview with author, November 20, 2020.
74. Asha Shipman, interview with author, November 15, 2020.

now using these physical practices to gain a proximity to Christ.'... So I sent him a little message and they removed the two lines... [Those who do this] rip out [yoga's original] spiritual teachings and replace it with the Bible."[75]

In Sharan's mind, simply being born Hindu is not enough to make one eligible for spiritual leadership in the Hindu community. It is a combination of personal practice and commitment as well as education in the deep meanings of Hindu philosophies—through a postcolonial lens that is not shaped by Western thought, whether that shows up as nationalism or Marxism as both are results of colonialism in his mind. Sharan suggests the solution to such deracination of the traditions is education: "The solution is education, but with that ... postcolonial theory has to sit front and center. With the education comes the actual practice of being a Hindu person or a spiritual person, 'Hindu' being just a word that means 'Indian.' They need to be part of the Dharmic tradition somehow. They have to have had some kind of teaching and guiding on the basis of ancient teachings from a spiritual teacher."[76]

Lastly there are other practical concerns that limit the full potential of Hindu chaplaincy today—they include the compensation of chaplains, lean program budgets, and the lack of time and inability to undertake professional development and program preparation. Regarding compensation, Shipman said, "I don't think [many chaplains] are paid living wages as chaplains. That's actually a huge struggle, too, in order to recruit people into the job. I can foresee recruiting someone really young. I cannot perceive recruiting someone who has a family, and whose entire family has to survive on the income that they get from chaplaincy. I don't see it. Not unless you're up higher. And even then, I'm not even sure. I don't know."[77] This was a challenge expressed by most of chaplains from traditions beyond Christianity and Judaism—that they are providing a crucial service in terms of making the campus hospitable and serving as mentors and advisors for students, and yet their compensation does not seem equitable to other university positions.

In addition, in some programs the budgets are very tight. Brahmachari Sharan has used some of his pay for other duties to supplement the program budget of his office, since the program requires significant resources

75. Vrajvihari Sharan, interview with author, November 20, 2020.
76. Vrajvihari Sharan, interview with author, November 20, 2020.
77. Asha Shipman, interview with author, November 15, 2020.

for support.⁷⁸ The chaplains I interviewed estimated that program budgets of $15-20,000 per semester are needed for strong university programs, although few had that available to them. Related to the challenge of resources is a challenge of having enough time to fulfill the duties of chaplaincy and still find the time to recharge and refresh spiritually and professionally, which is crucial for providing high-quality spiritual care. Vineet Chander said, "If there are little snatches of free time or of downtime, when I can remember to do it, and when I have the energy to do it, there is my own spiritual practice and formation and study, because I realize, and I've been humbled to realize, I've got to have something to give."⁷⁹

Future

Looking to the future, those I interviewed expressed excitement and optimism about the future of Hindu chaplaincy in American higher education. Vineet Chander believes Hindu chaplaincy has a bright future, and one that will be different for his daughter, who is now 11, when she gets to college and perhaps explores or experiences the Hindu community there:

> I'm just thinking about how different her experience will be from mine . . . As someone with this hyphenated identity, but maybe a little bit further removed from that immigrant "stranger in a strange land" experience . . . I think there's challenges that come with that, but the more optimistic, hopeful side of me sees chaplaincy playing a huge role in that. I think identity formation, spiritual formation, faith development, emotional, social development, all of that, social justice. I feel like religious life, spiritual life, chaplaincy has so much to offer and will only continue to offer. And, and I'm so excited about that happening within the context of the Hindu-American community.⁸⁰

In part, it will be different, he said, because she will not be the first-generation child of immigrant parents, and perhaps therefore more settled, and Hindu chaplaincies may be more institutionalized by then as well.

Several of the Hindu chaplains reflected on how their programs might be able to grow and change with more time and resources to take root. With the time and resources to pursue them, chaplains could expand their

---

78. Vrajvihari Sharan, interview with author, November 20, 2020.
79. Vineet Chander, interview with author, November 20, 2020.
80. Vineet Chander, interview with author, November 20, 2020.

offerings and programs in ways that would be enriching for their campus communities. At Princeton, for instance, there is a Hindu alumni community, but there has not yet been the time to fully and deeply engage with them. "I think it's a great untapped sort of audience or group to work with," Chander said. "I do more with recent alums and try to connect with some of our alumni that predate me because now, I have 10 years of alums ... "[81] Similarly, Brahmachari spoke of hoping to include in his chaplaincy work more of the travel experiences that can be deeply spiritual, educational, and transformative, "I do want to do a spiritual journey. We've done Delhi. We've done Mumbai. We were more looking at charity and social issues. But for the spiritual journey, I want to start in India, go through Nepal, and follow it to Cambodia and maybe even Bali. But it would be an entire fifteen-day trip, not for tourism, but for spiritual deepening in places that are potent beacons of dharmic heritage."[82]

Looking across the country, there are many regions that have been centers for Hindu and South Asian immigration where Hindu chaplaincies are not yet established. "There are institutions in states where there are more Hindus," Asha Shipman said. "And I actually found a listing at some point of the top ten institutions Indian-Americans want to go to .... [And most of the Hindu chaplains there are] all volunteers, which is ridiculous."[83] Having institutions establish more of these chaplaincies is an issue of equity, she suggested: "Framing it in a way right now that captures the national movements [for social justice], I think, is the way to do it. To basically say, look. Look at what's happening around you. There is systemic inequality in our institutions. That's not saying that you're awful, evil people, but there is systemic inequality. And there are resources. There are resources that can be used to correct this."[84]

Beyond but related to the Hindu community and Hindu chaplaincy is the question of chaplaincies for the distinct but historically and culturally related traditions of Sikhism and Jainism. At Georgetown, this was part of the reason Brahmachari Sharan advocated that his position be understood as supporting Dharmic Life: "When I got here, I realized that we have Buddhist students, we have Jain students, we have Sikh students—none of whom can have access to the kind of resources that the Hindus can, just

---

81. Vineet Chander, interview with author, November 20, 2020.
82. Vrajvihari Sharan, interview with author, November 20, 2020.
83. Asha Shipman, interview with author, November 15, 2020.
84. Asha Shipman, interview with author, November 15, 2020.

because [Hindus] have been advocating for it longer."[85] At Yale, Asha Shipman commented that more Jain students attend her programming and that Sikh students have recently organized and connect into the chaplain's office in a new way.[86] Regarding the Jain population, several have connected with the resources of the Hindu chaplaincy over time, given the overlap in philosophy and practice; and while they have not requested special accommodations, they have appreciated the support:

> One of my biggest supporters at Yale has been a Jain librarian. She's been amazing, she and her husband. And I actually, for Diwali Puja, I was like, "Okay, we've got to have a particular dish that doesn't have the onions and the garlic." And she was like, "You didn't have to do that for us."[87]

At Princeton, Chander said that as far as he knows, the Jain population has never had its own student group, and at various times has been more or less affiliated with the Hindu student group. He said he has connected with Jain students who at some level, spiritually or culturally, connect with the Hindu student community, although he is careful not to subsume their identity.[88] At Princeton, the Sikh community has been quite active although numerically small. But they have been visible, offering Sikh Awareness Days, offering *langars* (free community meals open to all), and bringing guest speakers to campus. Chander is himself Punjabi on his father's side and has both Hindus and Sikhs in his family. He has worn a Sikh *kara* bracelet at all times since he was a child, given that his family honors both traditions. Some Princeton students too have identified as both Hindu and Sikh. Although Chander said relations are always warm and cordial on a personal level, because of nationalist movements in South Asia, he has been sensitive about how he has approached extending various offerings, out of respect.[89]

Attention to and the importance of postcolonialism in higher education suggests that chaplaincy could be an important way to continue to address the postcolonial situation of contemporary times. Brahmachari Sharan believes that chaplains can be a kind of "threshold keeper," aware

---

85. Vrajvihari Sharan, interview with author, November 20, 2020.

86. Asha Shipman, email with author, March 25, 2021.

87. Asha Shipman, interview with author, November 15, 2020; Asha Shipman, email with author, March 25, 2021.

88. Vineet Chander, interview with author, November 20, 2020.

89. Vineet Chander, interview with author, November 20, 2020.

of important issues, dynamics, and discussions and able to help facilitate points of entry to them.[90] He said of chaplains, "They're able to speak to, and obviously they're not going to be experts in everything, but they would know who you should be chatting with. They should be aware of the current discussions in various communities. So, in terms of what it means to the university, yes, it means that [by having chaplains of different faiths present and available to support students], they would be dealing with decolonization in a very meaningful, palpable way."[91] In his view, and the view of the other chaplains doing this work, Sharan said,

> A really well-trained Hindu chaplain can be a very strong partner in all of the discussions around diversity, inclusion, equity. They can be very strong partners in helping the university understand the complexities of South Asia, given that one-third of the world lives there. .... More importantly, given that a lot of the foreign investment in terms of student dollars that come into universities are coming from South Asia, and Southeast Asia as well, . . . someone who really knows their stuff should also know enough to help navigate Southeast Asia and, to a point, the dharmic traditions that survive in China and Japan.[92]

---

90. Vrajvihari Sharan, interview with author, November 20, 2020.
91. Vrajvihari Sharan, interview with author, November 20, 2020.
92. Vrajvihari Sharan, interview with author, November 20, 2020.

3

Buddhist Chaplaincy

History

THE HISTORY OF BUDDHISM in America has developed in waves, from the Buddhism that Chinese and Japanese immigrants brought with them to Hawai'i and the West Coast of the United States during the Gold Rush in the mid-1800s, to the Buddhist influences on American Transcendentalist authors like Ralph Waldo Emerson and Henry David Thoreau in the 1850s, to lectures by Asian Buddhist leaders at the Chicago Parliament of the World's Religions in 1893. Then there were the Buddhist influences on the Beat Generation and the counterculture of the 1960s, and the Buddhism brought by newer waves of immigrants to the U.S. after the 1965 Immigration and Naturalization Act that helped open the doors for a new wave of Asian immigration to the United States.[1] Because of and through these various waves, there have been various examples of Buddhist presence and influences on American higher education.

For example, the Providence Zen Center was founded by Zen Master Seung Sahn, who immigrated from Korea to the U.S. in 1972, and, with no money and no knowledge of English, worked as a washing machine repairman in Providence, RI. While in Providence, Seung Sahn met a Brown University professor of Buddhism named Leo Pruden who invited him to give lectures at the university, after which students asked Seung Sahn to continue teaching them at his apartment. As more followers gathered, they came together to form the Providence Zen Center in 1979. A few years later in 1985, Seung Sahn founded the Kwan Um School of Zen, which now has

---

1. Pluralism Project, "Buddhism in America."

34 centers in the U.S. and 57 centers worldwide and is still headquartered in Rhode Island. The Kwan Um School blends Korean and American aspects of Buddhism.[2]

The story of Buddhism in America has many such connections between Buddhism and higher education at many major universities that have had connections with local Buddhist teachers and centers, through Buddhist faculty and staff members and interested students. As greater numbers of Asian and Asian American students have become students in American institutions of higher education in recent decades, these students have also brought with them traditions of Buddhism from their countries and families. Many universities and colleges across the country have had Buddhist and mindfulness student organizations for years, and many have more recently adopted secular meditation and mindfulness programs as part of their campus mental health and wellness initiatives.

However, few universities have Buddhist chaplaincies at the full-time or even part-time level. Only in recent years have Buddhist chaplaincy training programs been established at Harvard Divinity School, Union Theological Seminary, the University of the West, and the Naropa Institute. This timeline in the establishment of Buddhist chaplaincies may reflect a variety of factors, including the lack of national organizations to promote and establish Buddhist campus ministry positions at colleges and universities, and the fact that Buddhist practice in America has sometimes emphasized individual meditation over practices like rituals and community building. In any case, the presence of a Buddhist chaplaincy in American higher education, until very recently at just a few institutions like Wellesley College, Tufts, and Emory, has mostly involved Buddhist teachers who are volunteers or paid only minimal stipends to lead meditation on campus once or twice a week. While this has been helpful for the opportunities to practice meditation it has offered, it has also meant that Buddhism on campus has often lacked the visibility, the resources, and the intentional and robust community experiences that other religious traditions have had on campus.

The three Buddhist higher education chaplains I interviewed represent the different forms Buddhist chaplaincy has taken in higher education, from The Reverend Doyeon Park, who is a resident teacher at a Korean Won Buddhist Center in Manhattan and serves as an unpaid affiliated Buddhist spiritual life advisor at Columbia University and the first such advisor

---

2. Pluralism Project, "Providence Zen Center."

at NYU two days per week; to The Venerable Upali Sraman, a Bangladeshi Therevada Buddhist monk who served as a Harvard Divinity School Buddhist chaplaincy intern and then as a resident (undertaking a temporary supervised professional experience) at Tufts University; to Kotatsu John Bailes, an American convert to Japanese Zen Buddhism who is an ordained Buddhist priest and has served for seven years as the part-time Buddhist chaplain at Wellesley College.

The Reverend Doyeon Parks' story represents a typical way in which Buddhist teachers have come to be connected with colleges and universities. She says:

> I have my temple here in Manhattan, Won Buddhism of Manhattan. So, from the Won Buddhist tradition, we get assignments to the different temples. So, first, I was assigned to this local temple here in Manhattan in 2008. And then I've been here, working with my local community. And maybe around 2010, I got an email from the Columbia University Buddhist Association asking if I could come as a guest teacher. So, I went . . . I gave some teachings, and since then, they kind of invited me again, so maybe I went there, like on a monthly basis for a year. Now, one day their student leaders asked me if I was interested in becoming a Buddhist chaplain at Columbia. I was like wow, that sounds cool. And then I learned that, at that time, they had a Buddhist chaplain before me. But for a couple of years, somehow, they didn't have a [Buddhist] chaplain at Columbia. So, the student leaders, they recommended me to the chaplain's office.[3]

At Tufts University, when I went to serve there as university chaplain in 2013, there had been a Tufts Buddhist Sangha student organization for some decades, that met for weekly meditation and occasional retreats, supported by a local community member volunteer who was a convert to Buddhism. But I had the sense that Buddhism and mindfulness should be an important, central, and integrated part of the university chaplaincy, along with the other traditions Tufts had chaplains for at the time, which were Protestantism, Catholicism, Judaism, and Islam. And so, knowing of the new Buddhist Chaplaincy Initiative at Harvard Divinity School (HDS), I contacted HDS and asked if we could be a field education site for an intern in Buddhist chaplaincy. I then recruited The Venerable Upali Sraman, who became a part of our university chaplaincy staff and began to offer meditation and discussions twice per week in Goddard Chapel, to provide

---

3. Doyeon Park, interview with author, November 17, 2020.

pastoral care, and to participate in the interfaith activities of the office—giving public invocations, speaking at our revived Interfaith Student Council and first-year interfaith pre-orientation program, and sponsoring events such as a first-ever Buddha's Birthday Celebration at Tufts.

When Venerable Upali left to pursue his Ph.D. at Emory, I hired another recent graduate of HDS's Buddhist chaplaincy program, also a Bengali Theravada Buddhist monk, to continue the program, The Venerable Priya Rakkhit Sraman. Venerable Priya incorporated new elements, such as a connection with Harvard's Buddhism and Race Conference, off-site student retreats at the Wonderwell Mountain Refuge in New Hampshire, and more outreach to local teachers and Tufts alumni. The Buddhist community began to thrive and become a central part of the chaplaincy and a deeply important community for the students involved to learn, grow, and find wellbeing and peace. As Venerable Upali said:

> In 2013, when I came to the U.S., before that I had no idea about chaplaincy... I remember the use of the word, "chaplain" in some Buddhist texts as an advisor to the king, ... But I had no idea what chaplaincy looks like in the modern context, in the university, or even hospital. I haven't seen them in Sri Lanka or in Asia, for example. So when I was a master's student at the Harvard Divinity School, I learned about this word, "chaplaincy" ... and it was part of my curious mind to see what is it, chaplains? What do the chaplains do? And that's when the opportunity to intern at Tufts came up, so I was like, "Okay, I can give it a try." Originally, I was recommending some of my friends, I forwarded the advertisement to some of my friends who I thought are better capable of that. I was only one year in the U.S. by that point, so I was not brave enough to experiment at that time, but then they were pointing it back to me ... [and] said, "No, you can do it, and you should give it a try." So when I started, I had no idea what my duties are, so it was like learning an art by doing it kind of thing, so I was learning what is a chaplain by actually getting into it, and doing it without having much prior knowledge about it. So ... that is how I got to start it, yeah. And I learned many things on the way ...[4]

Along these lines, Wellesley College's multifaith chaplaincy, which was a prototype for the Tufts university chaplaincy, began in 1993 and hired a Buddhist chaplain 20 years before Tufts. They have now had several Buddhist chaplains, and the program has developed and changed over the

---

4. Upali Sraman, interview with author, November 13, 2020.

years. When the current Buddhist chaplain, Kotatsu John Bailes began, as he said:

> Victor [Kazanjian, the dean of religious life who implemented Wellesley's multifaith model] had left, things were in disarray, I was hired, and everything seemed somewhat chaotic. But I tend to be a person who chaos doesn't faze too much, and I just started, I had no direction, and there are very few Buddhists at Wellesley. So literally, I had to do a couple of things. One was continue a weekly meditation, which included people from outside of the Wellesley community, a group of people who I've been sitting with for these seven years every Monday evening at 5:00. It varies anywhere from 15 to 25, that are just adults living in Wellesley, Needham .... Some students would come to that. And then I started some student meditations, very sparsely attended. But I would just wander around the campus and smile and say hi to people. I've walked into the dining halls and things like this, and just start talking with people and things like that, and it was well received.[5]

Over time, Bailes, who also practices Tai Chi and Qigong, developed a connection with the physical education department, and with the support of then dean of religious life Tiffany Steinwert, was able to begin teaching Physical Education courses on meditation to students for course credit. These classes have since evolved into Bailes offering a number of other curricular and cocurricular connections that have helped to integrate the Buddhist chaplaincy program into the life of the college.[6]

While his training was as a Soto Zen priest for 12 years and in antinuclear weapons advocacy, and not in chaplaincy per se, Bailes had experience of American higher education from his undergraduate degree at Harvard and some graduate studies that helped him to make these institutional connections. His vision is one that was echoed in various ways by all three Buddhist chaplains. As Bailes put it,

> In the tradition I come from, I was taught, it doesn't matter whether you're a Buddhist, a Christian or a Jew. If you do these practices they'll make you a better, they'll help you be a better human being, which is a better Christian, Jew, Muslim, Buddhist, whatever. So I didn't have too much hang up on just appearing as the Buddhist guy running around doing Buddhist things, as much as I was feeling for what the students required, and then how to fill that need

---

5. John Bailes, interview with author, November 23, 2020.
6. John Bailes, interview with author, November 23, 2020.

if you will, sensitively, and without what I'll call disregarding the central fact that I'm a Buddhist.[7]

Venerable Upali shared a similar idea:

> And we have been seeing that, I think from the beginning, when Buddhism came a couple of hundred years ago, but even more so now than before, is that there is something in Buddhism about helping others. So it is within the structure of Buddhism, self-benefit and other benefits. So that's kind of the basic structure of Buddhism. What are you doing for another person, whether it is just sharing a good uplifting verse from something, like encouraging someone or giving a good smile or something that makes another person happy . . . giving some support to someone. So in all these virtues that it talks about, it's not who identifies as a Buddhist. It's about what is it that you're doing for another person in the way that you are moving around. And it goes as far as just creating a safe space for other people, it doesn't have to be necessarily that you are directly interacting with another person and then teaching them something, but it's just creating a safe space. And I think that is why students from different communities find interest in Buddhism and they get attracted to Buddhist clubs is that, you don't have to be a Buddhist . . . So the thing is, what kind of space you create around yourself in the way that, are you making it safe for other people to be there?[8]

Preparation

An interesting common thread among all the Buddhist chaplains I interviewed is that they expressed it does not matter how "Buddhist" their work and programs are as much as whether they are spreading and cultivating Buddhist values such as caring, friendship, and loving-kindness. As Venerable Upali said, "All of [the Buddhist teachers who come to the Emory Buddhist Club] are trained in traditional monastic settings, but they can still relate to the people because it's at the core that their purpose is to show what they can do for another person. So how Buddhism is communicated to the student is reflected in that. So they're like intending, how can I say something that is actually beneficial for another person?"[9]

---

7. John Bailes, interview with author, November 23, 2020.
8. Upali Sraman, interview with author, November 13, 2020.
9. Upali Sraman, interview with author, November 13, 2020.

As simple as that may sound, it is significant that all of the Buddhist chaplains I interviewed and, as Venerable Upali said, all of the teachers that lead meditation and discussion at the Emory Buddhist Club are trained in traditional Buddhist education systems.[10] This seems to be common among Buddhist chaplains, and it is significant because it indicates that usually some level of traditional Buddhist practice and training is a prerequisite for effective Buddhist chaplaincy. As Kotatsu John Bailes of Wellesley College said, "One has to be grounded in the actual practice, not the intellectual study. To hire someone . . . if they haven't had the practice, if they've just . . . got their M.Div. in Buddhist stuff, my experience . . . is although they're intelligent and well meaning, it's all head stuff. What I mean by that is, it's all ideas about how things ought to be if you were a Buddhist."[11]

This raises an interesting point that the preparation, training, and learning necessary to be a Buddhist teacher or chaplain does not come primarily through Western education alone. All three Buddhist chaplains I interviewed had a level of traditional training, as The Reverend Doyeon Park said,

> different Buddhist traditions have different kinds of ways to become a teacher. So particularly in [the Korean Won] tradition, let's say, I had like a first two years of novice training period, where I lived with my mentor teacher in her temple in Korea . . . .and then I have four years of undergrad programs in Korea. And there's two more years of graduate programs here in the United States. So, there's six years because I took a year off somewhere between. It took almost like ten years to finish all the trainings and programs and be fully ordained.[12]

Kotatsu John Bailes had a similar, twelve-year traditional training, "I don't have advanced degrees . . . But from the president on down, they respect the fact that I'm an ordained, fully-empowered Soto Zen Buddhist priest, and I have these robes that I can pull out, and I appear to have some practice, some way of being with people and I think they respect that tremendously."[13]

In addition to traditional Buddhist training, all three Buddhist chaplains also spoke about the importance of understanding American higher

---

10. Upali Sraman, interview with author, November 13, 2020.
11. John Bailes, interview with author, November 23, 2020.
12. Doyeon Park, interview with author, November 17, 2020.
13. John Bailes, interview with author, November 23, 2020.

education for knowing how best to translate and integrate Buddhist teachings into the college or university. For The Reverend Doyeon Park at NYU, as a spiritual life advisor, some of this learning has come through regular affiliate meetings with the Office of Global Spiritual Life. She said,

> In the beginning, I only took this as an opportunity to meet with the students and to teach Buddhism and meditation. Even today, that's . . . the main thing for me. But then joining the schools' chaplains' teams, I think every year I find more responsibility. One thing I really like about the chaplaincy is that, at Columbia University and New York University, we have monthly meetings, we have some orientation meetings, so that they inform us what's going on at the university level, and then what they are expecting from us. And then, for me, that's also a lot of good education.[14]

Park expressed this has helped her be effective in bringing her training from the Won tradition into the university, "In order for us to serve the students well, then we need to know what the needs are and what's going on with the students. So, I really appreciate the different educational aspects I get from the schools. I've been getting more understanding of, it started with first LGBT community, now LGBTQ community, and now LGBTQIA . . . So, I'm learning all these things to be more aware of what the students' needs are."[15] Kotatsu John Bailes has had a mix of Western and traditional Buddhist education and training, and he spoke of his ability to navigate such institutions.[16] And Venerable Upali spoke of starting at Tufts and being part of the university chaplaincy team there as a way to learn how to provide effective chaplaincy.[17]

There are of course now several programs at U.S. universities and divinity schools that offer training for Buddhist chaplaincy. The Reverend Doyeon Park was aware of these programs but wondered how many Buddhist chaplaincy opportunities there are for their graduates, and in what institutions, given that at least in higher education, most positions have been volunteer or part time.[18] Venerable Upali did attend one of these programs for his M.Div. at Harvard Divinity School, which was additional to his

---

14. Doyeon Park, interview with author, November 17, 2020.
15. Doyeon Park, interview with author, November 17, 2020.
16. John Bailes, interview with author, November 23, 2020.
17. Upali Sraman, interview with author, November 13, 2020.
18. Doyeon Park, interview with author, November 17, 2020.

traditional Buddhist training. He spoke of the main value of this program being training in pastoral care,

> So we had some requirements fortunately for the M.Div. program that were actually focused on chaplaincy practices. And I'm so glad and grateful I did go through those courses. There were some courses on pastoral care and . . . I think just the practice of ministry . . . And I also took a course on Buddhist chaplaincy. So in all of these classes, active listening was very strongly emphasized. . . . And we had sessions where we would do almost like mock counseling, where we would pretend that someone is a patient or just a student sharing something, and then we have to pretend we are the counselors listening to them.[19]

Additionally, Venerable Upali said he has found training in active listening most helpful, "So all of those courses really helped me, and really, my mind got stuck in the active listening part. This is so crucial. And I think that it's so important in all forms of relationship, but especially for those who are in caregiving practices, in whatever forms, active listening is so important."[20] Other chaplains also shared that a U.S. degree added a kind of recognition of their training that is valued by institutions of higher education as employers, since traditional training may not be fully understood.

One question that remains as Buddhist chaplain positions become available and people apply for or are nominated or recruited for these roles is the relative benefits of being a monastic teacher or a lay teacher, of being "robed" or "unrobed." On the one hand, the robe can be a mark of traditional education and authority to teach, and also ideally a sign that one is living the practice. On the other hand, people do not always know how to treat monastics, and some monastics have wondered whether a robe when not understood may become a kind of a barrier.[21] Indeed, some monastics wearing robes have even been the targets of prejudice and discrimination. Kotatsu John Bailes felt that his robe has been effective in communicating training and teaching authority,[22] but Venerable Upali shared that he wondered the following:

> [Are] U.S. universities prepared to have monastics in major kind of institutional roles? . . . Lay Buddhists have this additional challenge

19. Upali Sraman, interview with author, November 13, 2020.
20. Upali Sraman, interview with author, November 13, 2020.
21. Upali Sraman, interview with author, November 13, 2020.
22. John Bailes, interview with author, November 23, 2020.

of proving themselves because even though they may have a lot of wisdom, but they don't have the robe, so people sometimes, within the tradition, don't take them seriously as proper authorities. Especially for ritualistic kind of things. . . . But also I think if there is a [different] kind of institution, for example, how open are they to accept actual monastic figures as chaplains in the positions . . . . I'm not sure . . . So I think this is something to think about. How do people accept Buddhist monks as chaplains?[23]

Venerable Upali was pursuing his Ph.D. and considering university teaching roles, and he wondered how widely monastics would be accepted into such faculty roles, especially if robed.[24] In light of this, it seems that as Buddhism takes its place in American higher education, there are multiple questions of navigation and negotiation between traditional practices and what is expected or believed to be effective in the American higher education context, with respect to preferred educational background, engagement in the institution, and the signs of leadership.

Responsibilities

An interesting question about Buddhism on college and university campuses that builds on the question of how campuses welcome and receive Buddhist monastics and teachers is the question of how Buddhism is being presented on campus. Buddhism is an ancient, large, diverse, and complex tradition with many branches and sects, even within the three broad divisions of Theravada, Mahayana, and Vajrayana, as well as many ethnic manifestations from different countries. In terms of Buddhist leadership, campuses have tended to have one of two models—either they have no Buddhist chaplain, and they regularly invite in different teachers to teach each week, or they may have a Buddhist advisor or chaplain who provides regular Buddhist teaching, but who may also invite in other teachers as guests for occasional lectures or rituals. There are several potential downsides of inviting in many Buddhist teachers without a consistent chaplaincy presence. One is that without a regular chaplain, there is no professional leader to really cultivate the community, provide continuity, and offer consistent and reliable pastoral care and other support.[25] Also, a revolving door of

23. Upali Sraman, interview with author, November 13, 2020.
24. Upali Sraman, interview with author, November 13, 2020.
25. Upali Sraman, interview with author, November 13, 2020.

teachers might suggest that Buddhism is only about meditation and meditation instruction, rather than building a spiritual community that would engage in various kinds of spiritual practices, including religious, educational, pastoral, service, social justice, and community-building programs.

Another potential downside to this rotating model of visiting teachers is that all of the teachers may tend to generalize their teachings into a kind of generic and introductory Buddhism, because they understand that they are teaching to a community that is diverse and not their usual congregation, and they want to be accessible and be of service to the campus.[26] Venerable Upali said students have sometimes expressed that they want to go deeper into Buddhist teachings, and they feel each week with rotating teachers is a kind of "introduction to meditation." This approach can have both positive and negative aspects. On the one hand, it can create a kind of "ecumenical Buddhism," where there can be unity among many branches and schools that otherwise might not be the case.[27] This has often happened when minority religious traditions take hold in the U.S.—when adherents are fewer in numbers, distinctions of sect or language may fall away in a desire for a larger community. On the other hand, it can erase some of the rich distinctiveness of particular Buddhist traditions, and even make a Buddhist club's activities unrecognizable to adherents who are used to certain forms.

Venerable Upali Sraman described the type of Buddhism that seems to be developing in this way as perhaps a new branch or sect, called "College Buddhism." He said,

> I have a lot of curiosity and interest in what they call the 'College Buddhism,' how college students are shaping a new kind of Buddhism in a new way. So, we have the traditional Buddhist communities in the U.S., like people coming from Asia, Sri Lanka and Vietnam, Myanmar, Cambodia—they have their own monasteries for example, and they do their own things. And sometimes the traditional Buddhist communities themselves don't have much opportunity to interact with each other . . . or they are not curious about interacting with each other because they have what they want within their own community.[28]

On campus however, there can be a kind of melting pot effect:

---

26. Upali Sraman, interview with author, November 13, 2020.
27. Upali Sraman, interview with author, November 13, 2020.
28. Upali Sraman, interview with author, November 13, 2020.

> But the students from all those communities come to university, and then now we have a place where students from Chinese, Tibetan, or Southeast Asian communities who are all part of the Buddhist student community . . . are kind of exploring each other among the students themselves. I think even in places where you don't have an institutionalized Buddhist chaplain, the students themselves somehow find a way to interact, and then discover each other, and discover Buddhism in a new way, so that itself is fascinating.[29]

Of course, as is true of all religious traditions, no single chaplain can embody within themselves all of the diverse branches and ritual forms of any tradition, but they can learn to be a coordinator and connector to various particular resources. Coming together can provide a beautiful opportunity for mutual learning and enhanced perspective, but it can create the challenge of losing distinctiveness. As Venerable Upali said:

> I think that what is emerging through . . . 'College Buddhism,' it's the gist of Buddhism that people are finding ways to connect to everyone . . . despite our cultural differences and language differences. . . . [But] sometimes it's too simplistic; everyone is kind of shooting for mindfulness as the only thing that connects . . . I think that's simplifying the complexity of Buddhism in that way. . . . You see all the guest teachers coming from all these different traditions are all talking about mindfulness. But if you go to each of their monasteries, I don't think you'll hear that that's what they talk about when they are addressing their own communities, they talk about so many other things. So . . . students . . . like to say that, 'Oh, we have different teachers from all different traditions.' That's good, but they don't say that all teachers are saying the same thing.[30]

Coordinating and curating the internal diversity of the tradition so that students have a consistent experience of community as well as opportunities to learn about and connect with diverse traditions and teachings within Buddhism can be an important role of the Buddhist chaplain—providing communication among various teachers, etc. A benefit of a variety of teachers as well is that they can provide additional diversity of leadership, in terms of gender, race, and ethnicity, as well as the traditions within Buddhism. And having some introduction to off-campus Buddhist centers

---

29. Upali Sraman, interview with author, November 13, 2020.
30. Upali Sraman, interview with author, November 13, 2020.

can help students to go deeper into Buddhist practice if they wish through off-campus retreats, or when they need to find a Buddhist community off-campus when they graduate.

At Tufts, one way that the Buddhist chaplains have provided more contextual or particular forms of Buddhist experience, beyond weekly meditations and discussions, has been by adding opportunities to do other forms of practice, such as chanting, or full moon ceremonies, and also through observances such as celebrating the Buddha's Birthday. When asked why he created Tufts' first Buddha Day celebration, Venerable Upali Sraman said:

> We are all talking about Buddhism in the first place because of the Buddha. So he is the master par excellence of this. So, I think in some ways it's not different from all the major days, connected to distinguished personalities in the world. It's just a way to celebrate his teaching, his life, that because of him, we are doing all these practices for our mental wellbeing and emotional wellbeing.[31]

In addition, he described that organizing larger, more visible events than regular meditation gatherings offered other benefits, such as providing entry points into the program, and allowing the students to use their creativity and develop their leadership skills. He said, "I realized that having a holiday observance is actually good because . . . of how students feel interested and excited about being a member of the organization by organizing events. So, students feel some kind of agency and excitement, 'Oh, we are part of a good event and we want to do it.'" This can be an important learning experience:

> So, I think having a Vesak Day at least or a day like that, at least once a year, I would say to organize more of these kind of events is good based on the students' interest. . . . There is a lot of leadership going on so they can show some of their own creativity in this. So, it's not only about the Buddha and just the religious part of it. But also I realize that the students like to showcase some of their creativity and leadership skills in that, and to organize an event like that is an opportunity for them actually to do that.[32]

In addition, a moment such as Vesak or the Buddha's Birthday provides an opportunity for interfaith dialogue, learning, and engagement. In the Buddha's Birthday celebrations at Tufts, for instance, Venerable Upali

---

31. Upali Sraman, interview with author, November 13, 2020.
32. Upali Sraman, interview with author, November 13, 2020.

Sraman invited other chaplains, faculty members, staff, and students to speak about themes that related to Buddhist values, such as nonviolence, harmony, generosity, and compassion. All of the Buddhist chaplains stressed that interfaith work and ceremonies are important aspects of their work. Along these lines, The Reverend Doyeon Park said:

> One other very important thing is participating in interfaith [engagement]. That's also a big part of my work at each school. Maybe from the interfaith programs from the university chaplain's office, or different student groups or schools, different departments, they organize interfaith gatherings. And whenever I get the invitation, I always try to be there. It's in a way to show that the Buddhist chaplain is available and here for the greater people.[33]

Kotatsu John Bailes spoke about how such interfaith moments at Wellesley College—Flower Sunday as students arrive, and Baccalaureate as students depart—provide opportunities for building and celebrating friendships, supporting one another, and growing as a community. He said,

> For what we call Flower Sunday, which is our bringing together the first years and meeting the community, there'll be 800 students in the chapel. And at Baccalaureate, again, there'll be 800 students in the chapel, and they'll be sharing. They're not all goodie goodies, they have some critical things to say when they speak and so on. But they cheer and they support one another, and they recognize the difficulty that they've all gone through somehow, together at Wellesley. . . . This is really, really important. I thought, "My God, this is really great. How do we foster this sense of awareness and bonds?"[34]

Some of these interfaith moments and public ceremonies help to raise the visibility of spiritual life and Buddhist life as resources for students, and they also provide rituals that shape the community. The Venerable Upali Sraman also described the benefits of showing up at Muslim Jumu'ah Prayer, or at the Tufts Interfaith Student Council, or participating with other chaplains in more significant interfaith programs, such the Tufts interfaith social justice pre-orientation program, CAFÉ.[35] Having so many different communities, in such close proximity, actively open to all, and within the overarching community of a single campus, allows for interfaith learning

---

33. Doyeon Park, interview with author, November 17, 2020.
34. John Bailes, interview with author, November 23, 2020.
35. Upali Sraman, interview with author, November 13, 2020.

and engagement in a unique way. It builds opportunities to appreciate differences as well as to identify common purposes, that can lead to solidarity and positive social change. Venerable Upali Sraman said,

> I think it's really good to have these opportunities for interfaith education. I think that the benefit of the interfaith gatherings I find is ... you see each religion talking in their own voice ... it tells us how we can use different languages and different beliefs. We can come from different belief systems, but then we have a common purpose ... So that's why I find the beauty of these interfaith gatherings. We can come from different places, but still, you can stand for one purpose.[36]

As Kotatsu John Bailes suggests, this interfaith community building can lead to a kind of effective advocacy for institutional and social change that builds relationships and capacity rather than tension and animosity. He said,

> I do things like show up for a group called EnAct, and they're the students working on climate change. In my work outside, I support groups like ... Extinction Rebellion ... the climate group that started in England that does civil disobedience, peaceful disobedience. I provide support and do group meditations with them and things like that. But that's a way of being engaged and it's a way of supporting the students and questioning. I can't say well, you should do these things, but they organize petitioning the president and the board about [fossil fuel] divestment and all of this stuff that's important, and important for them to find out that A) they can do that, and B) they could actually do it in a way that doesn't create animosity. . . . I think we chaplains fall into this place where we're helping create this bridge, and so that's a lot of the work I do, too. I work with First Generation and also Black students and students from other parts of the world like Las Cruces, NM, which can seem as far as Beijing.[37]

All of the Buddhist chaplains I interviewed described offering vibrant Buddhist life programs for their campus communities—usually rooted in a program of leading weekly meditation and discussions, being available for pastoral care, providing spiritual advice to the Buddhist student organization, and helping to connect students with resources offered by local Buddhist centers, such as retreats. That is the core of the work that The

---

36. Upali Sraman, interview with author, November 13, 2020.
37. John Bailes, interview with author, November 23, 2020.

Reverend Doyoen Park offers on campus at Columbia and NYU as an affiliate advisor.[38] When The Venerable Upali Sraman started at Tufts, his duties were similar. Having started by leading meditation, it soon became evident that discussions, or dharma talks, were also as desired by the students as meditation: "One [day] was to practice . . . and then afterwards, experience sharing and question and answer. Then another day was for a normal discussion where the practice was less, but more discussion. So, I would bring some passages to read, or I would encourage them to bring some passages. And then the discussion would be around whatever reading we shared."[39] In this way, not only were students growing in their practice of meditation, but also in their understanding of Buddhist teachings and their reflection on and incorporation of those teachings in their lives. And significantly, after the sessions the students also shared tea and snacks to build community.

Additionally, for all the Buddhist chaplains, pastoral care is an important part of their work. Venerable Upali Sraman found providing pastoral care was a significant part of his role. He said, "It is different. . . . from just having a meditation program. A meditation program by itself is helpful, but I think that . . . sometimes it's not actually the program itself or the content of what you talk about or what is being taught by a teacher. It's the person . . . that people want to relate to, to have a person who you think is a friend, who can present himself . . . in a pastoral care setting."[40] Venerable Upali Sraman spoke about this more accessible, and perhaps less structured model of support that chaplains offer, different from mental health counseling, as being deeply valuable. He said:

> My own experience of using the counseling facilities, . . . I have used that many times myself, but then there are certain things that are very kind of, how to say, the formalities of counseling, it kind of throws off people. So sometimes all the forms that I have to fill out and all those things, even before I could actually tell what is my issue, and I can talk about it, that I have to go through all those things. But maybe sometimes, psychologically, a person who needs some care, maybe just needs someone to talk to because they are feeling blue or something like that, when something terrible happened, not a major psychological issue, but something is

---

38. Doyeon Park, interview with author, November 17, 2020.
39. Upali Sraman, interview with author, November 13, 2020.
40. Upali Sraman, interview with author, November 13, 2020.

still urgent. That counseling is I think a little bit distant to provide that kind of care.[41]

Chaplaincy can be much more accessible, he said, for situations that are emotionally painful but not psychological crises, such as death and grief. "When a student passed away in a terrible accident, we had the chaplaincy service, so they could just send me an email, 'How are you, if you're on campus, you want to talk?' So I was actually able to say, 'I'm not on campus, but I can come to you. . . . . So, let's talk."[42]

In an even more robust program, such as the program that has developed at Wellesley College, Kotatsu John Bailes has been able to develop valuable connections with the faculty, curriculum, and courses that provide ways of integrating meditation, mindfulness, and Buddhist teaching more deeply into the academic mission.[43] When he came to Wellesley, after starting to lead weekly meditation and discussions, and working to survey the needs of the campus, he said,

> It felt to me . . . 'Well, what we need to do here is do something else.' We need to build a community of what I call loving-kindness, and an awareness of interdependence, and lay the groundwork for people to begin to think about these things.' And out of that I said, 'Well, I will organize a mindfulness course pilot,' and I looked around for stuff. The one I settled on to use as my core is Koru [Mindfulness] . . . . because it was designed by I think a psychologist and an M.D., and has a lot to do with emotional and physical and brain formation that's going on in people between 16 and 25 or so.[44]

Bailes was looking for something that might be more accessible and guided than his own practice, "So I come from the Zen school, . . . basically we just sit. So, I ring a bell, people sit. But sitting for 30 or 40 minutes without being told what to do or when to do it, or just being told, 'This is what we do,' and then left with your body and your breath for 30 or 40 minutes, an 18 or a 19 year old without any interest in Buddhism or something, doesn't know what to do, and it's quite strange and has no access."[45] Koru helped to provide a good base, "What I found is the Koru stuff as they

---

41. Upali Sraman, interview with author, November 13, 2020.
42. Upali Sraman, interview with author, November 13, 2020.
43. John Bailes, interview with author, November 23, 2020.
44. John Bailes, interview with author, November 23, 2020.
45. John Bailes, interview with author, November 23, 2020.

designed it for these 10 minute pieces and so on, and guided meditations and things like this, begins to get a toehold and a handhold into what actually being present and being able to give our attention and not be pulled away by our anxiety or restlessness or discomfort, how to be present over time with that."[46] A main part of the course Bailes now offers is focused on ways of accessing and enhancing the parasympathetic nervous system, which he describes:

> the sympathetic [nervous system] is adreno-cortical, everything that's out there that I'm worrying about and holding back and exhausting myself, and parasympathetic is nourishing. So it's physical—heart rate lowers, respiratory rate lowers, blood pressure lowers . . . Our sense of hand-eye coordination actually gets better and we have a sense of pleasing, we become more inclusive, warm, feel at home. We become more relaxed and resilient and buoyant. It's just nourishing to our entire being, let's put it that way.[47]

Through regular meditation practice in the course, Bailes seeks to teach accessing and tending to the parasympathetic system. In addition, he seeks to introduce students to or support them in building these practices into their lives, almost like in a monastic setting in which residents move "like a pod of whales" and "part of a larger organism."[48] He said this is about "harmonizing our life in some way through the other thing that students wake up to, [which] is routine or ritual. How do I wake up in the morning? How do I establish my day? How do I go to sleep at night, how do I change my frame of mind from the day running around and doing everything, sort of external push, to quieting so I can actually go to sleep?"[49] One of the important rhythms is the rhythm of sleep,

> We work on that a lot because, and I'm presuming this is across the board at what I'll call competitive colleges or higher education, that students don't sleep well. So, one of the most important things for me is to actually help them get to sleep, and to understand that they have something they can do. So, they begin to wake up to it in the mindfulness course, because of the regularity of it, a sense of agency in spaces, in what I'll call subjective spaces, where they generally lose themselves to their anxiety or depression or

---

46. John Bailes, interview with author, November 23, 2020.
47. John Bailes, interview with author, November 23, 2020.
48. John Bailes, interview with author, November 23, 2020.
49. John Bailes, interview with author, November 23, 2020.

negativity and find that they can actually make a choice . . . they could actually go for a walk or follow their breath."[50]

As a guest lecturer, Bailes also brings these practices into other university spaces, such as the writing program and the university museum, giving talks on meditation, mindfulness, and creativity and doing some exercises, offering guided meditations in the galleries so that people can "relax and open . . . let go of their cognitive interpretive world to experience the painting or the art in a . . . less obscured or more immediate fashion . . . Thirty people from the alumni, the community, the students and staff, attend that." And he has also been invited to lead such meditations to start meetings of the college's division of student life.[51]

The Reverend Doyeon Park at Columbia and NYU discussed being invited to give similar talks in some classes, such as in the Teachers College or the College of Physicians, although she noted, never in the religion courses.[52] The Venerable Upali Sraman also spoke about the complementary role that the Buddhist chaplain and the Buddhist life program can have with respect to the classroom, including courses on Buddhism.[53] In general, in courses on Buddhism, he said, "The professor has a limited role in the sense that they have a course that they have to teach. And it's mostly like the purpose is different. It's not to teach them to become great meditators for example."[54] There are sometimes exceptions, such as a course that he was a teaching assistant for on Contemplative Practices, "So we would meditate for about fifteen, twenty minutes before the class every day." But usually he said, "Buddhism is being introduced to students in a more academic way."[55] As a complement to those courses, Buddhist chaplains can have a different role: "introducing the culture and the ritual and the prayer styles. And also . . . the experience of the tradition in a more personal way, a transformative way . . . So that's something the chaplaincy is capable of but the professor does not have the opportunity and the space to do . . . . Once in a while, the professors would take students for ethnography trips, field trips, but that's not the same thing as having a chaplain."[56]

50. John Bailes, interview with author, November 23, 2020.
51. John Bailes, interview with author, November 23, 2020.
52. Doyeon Park, interview with author, November 17, 2020.
53. Upali Sraman, interview with author, November 13, 2020.
54. Upali Sraman, interview with author, November 13, 2020.
55. Upali Sraman, interview with author, November 13, 2020.
56. Upali Sraman, interview with author, November 13, 2020.

Challenges

When it comes to the challenges facing Buddhist chaplaincy in higher education today, some of them are common to other newer traditions to chaplaincy—such as a lack of history of chaplaincy leading to challenges of recognition, the part-time and less well compensated nature of some of these positions, the systemic inequality impacting the tradition that means that resources are less available, and the need for appropriate space for religious practice when that has not been part of past institutional plans, etc. And there are other issues particular to the tradition, such as misunderstandings of the tradition or cultural appropriation that cause it to be viewed as just meditation or mindfulness, as well as unique ways in which dynamics of race and divides between birth-Buddhists and converts can arise in Buddhist communities.

The Venerable Upali Sraman shared that the transition from unpaid part-time Buddhist advisors to paid professional Buddhist chaplains, when it has happened institutionally, has led to greater visibility and accessibility.[57] With a lack of history of Buddhist chaplaincy within the Buddhist tradition and within higher education, on many campuses Buddhist offerings and communities have begun informally, such as by students gathering to form a club. Occasionally they then begin to invite Buddhist teachers to come and lead them in meditation and discussions, and then eventually those leaders may become affiliates or advisors, as was the case for The Reverend Doyeon Park.[58]

But without having the status of paid professional chaplains, these leaders are not university employees and so they lack the visibility, access, and integration that other university staff members have, which means their programs and communities also lack visibility and integration. It can mean that the quality or regularity of the programs is less, or that the campus may have more difficulty knowing about and accessing the resource. It also limits the impact and influence of the Buddhist leader and the Buddhist community on the campus overall. As Venerable Upali Sraman said,

> The way I see it is that, having something institutionalized makes it more visible, I would say, compared to having something that the students are privately doing on their own, and the university has no idea who is the teacher, and who are these groups. And also it's

---

57. Upali Sraman, interview with author, November 13, 2020.
58. Doyeon Park, interview with author, November 17, 2020.

more limited; so it's mostly students who already know something about Buddhism and have some experience about Buddhist meditation, so I think they're the ones who make this arrangement. . . . So that's what happens, that's how usually things continue in a very small private group. But then having something institutionalized, I think makes it more visible, and it has more potential.[59]

Venerable Upali described how the visibility of these offerings, as featured and publicized by the Tufts university chaplaincy and taking place in Tufts' Goddard Chapel, became more of a resource: "So just to give one example is that, in my Buddhist Sangha, it was not only the Buddhist students who came . . . . but I had people from different religious communities; Hindus also came. And for the first time I met a person from the Baha'i community, [who] said his community is so small, or maybe he was the only person that he knew following the Baha'i faith there, so there was no place to go, [and] he would come to my meditations."[60] During my time as university chaplain at Tufts, our office made the Sangha known as a staff-supported university resource, which helped the campus realize it was there and truly open to everyone. It also allowed for visioning and goal setting with Buddhist chaplain, to include faculty and staff programs, etc. And having meditation cushions available in the chapel sanctuary made students' practice easier.

At the same time, few institutions have created Buddhist chaplaincies to date, which has implications for the viability of Buddhist chaplaincy as a field and for the forms programs can take. As is the case for Muslim, Hindu, and Humanist chaplaincy, the newness of the field in the tradition and in higher education means that there are not strong established national or international networks to support Buddhist chaplains, and so the positions that exist, when they do, are often part time, not highly compensated, may not offer benefits, and do not really allow time for expanding the program with opportunities like retreats, or opportunities for the chaplain to network or build professional associations. As Kotatsu John Bailes shared, when he started at Wellesley, he was considered to be in the category of a "casual employee."[61] In some cases, being part time may serve the spiritual life advisor well, if they have other more stable duties, such as in a center. However, this does not mean that the arrangement is really meeting the

---

59. Upali Sraman, interview with author, November 13, 2020.
60. Upali Sraman, interview with author, November 13, 2020.
61. John Bailes, interview with author, November 23, 2020.

fullness of the campus' needs in the best possible way. Venerable Upali Sraman felt that retreats would be very beneficial, but there was not time to develop them in his part-time hours:

> I remember when we were meeting, we would meet one-on-one. I would talk about [retreats], but then we couldn't really manage the time to do that, but that is something I think, is very important to have more of in the practice. Weekly meetings are . . . a time to break, take some deep breaths, relax a little bit, and have some pause during the week too, for reflection. But having some retreat experience, I think is crucial for the experience of meditation, but also for the students to experience Buddhism in a deeper way. I found myself that no matter how many books I read or how many lectures I have heard, there is nothing compared to a retreat. A meditation retreat is really good. We need that time for meditation and deeper reflection.[62]

Kotatsu John Bailes said retreats have also been a longtime hope of his but beyond reach: "Well . . . I keep thinking . . . maybe I could be there full time and then we could develop more continuity with all the people who've taken the class and so on. What happens when you're twenty hours a week or so, that all has to be looked at like, it's not so much it can't be done, but it's going to take four or five years to make something happen."[63] The combination of no or low pay and little time make such positions difficult in terms of what can be offered and the prospects of longevity.

As a minority tradition in the U.S., Buddhist practitioners also continue to face prejudice and discrimination, and that sometimes causes people to feel less free to be public about their Buddhist identities, which has the impact of stifling student advocacy for Buddhist resources. There is a sense that the numbers of self-identifying Buddhists on many campuses is small, although many more who might not identify probably practice meditation. It's possible, if Buddhist chaplaincy develops, like Muslim and Hindu chaplaincy, that it could have an influence on stereotype reduction. Venerable Upali said,

> That's I think why a chaplaincy is not only just an optional thing, but a necessary thing is that. . . . I have heard from people who identify as Buddhists, but then feel embarrassed to identify . . . that they are actually Buddhist. But they feel embarrassed, especially

---

62. Upali Sraman, interview with author, November 13, 2020.
63. John Bailes, interview with author, November 23, 2020.

in, primary schools and secondary schools when students are very mean to each other. In the college, I think students are a little more polite and they behave like adults. But in the schools, I think they tease each other. I have heard from friends who felt very ashamed and they felt it's like a crime actually, sometime that they feel a strong sense of guilt that they are Buddhist because of the way they get bullied by their classmates or students. So, because of the embarrassment, I think that many people maybe in an early part of their life don't identify as Buddhist, and then they kind of continue in that.[64]

Venerable Upali said he thinks that Buddhist chaplains could have a positive effect, as a visible leader and spokesperson of the community:

So having a chaplain who is Buddhist, I think there's that opportunity that they don't have to be ashamed. And talking about all kinds of chaplains, not only Buddhists, but to have that as a strong part of the campus, a strong presence of a person from their religion. I don't think that it will ever be possible to represent everyone, but still that's setting a fair step, a good step to just show that you don't have to hide your identity, you can be a Buddhist. Otherwise, it can be quite depressing to be someone and believe in something, but then not have a space to express that.[65]

The combination of prejudice and cultural dynamics may also mean that even if a Buddhist chaplain were understood to be a helpful resource, students might not advocate for it. As The Reverend Doyeon Park said, "Then like, internationally, especially, a lot of students from Asian countries, they are so much, except for the Christian community, . . . being so quiet. They're not really asking for their own needs, which are underrepresented . . . And then not even asking the school."[66]

One important resource, which is also needed in a special way to practice Islam and Hinduism, is appropriate sacred space for practicing, which often does not exist on campuses until it is designated or created. For the Buddhist community, a regular, quiet space is needed for meditation with an accessible storage area for cushions and other equipment. Not having such a regular and appropriate space can have a serious negative impact on program attendance. At Columbia, The Reverend Doyeon Park said,

---

64. Upali Sraman, interview with author, November 13, 2020.
65. Upali Sraman, interview with author, November 13, 2020.
66. Doyeon Park, interview with author, November 17, 2020.

our regular students attended in a much bigger group of about thirty or forty. But then, we had a couple years of a very big kind of transition with our student leaders and . . . miscommunication with the university. We had to move our meeting rooms every week. Think about it, we had to find a room every different week. So gradually, we lost a lot of students for a couple semesters with this unstable kind of meeting situation.[67]

The students initially decided to try changing rooms because they had been meeting in the basement of Columbia's Earl Hall on Thursday nights, but Thursday night being a popular night for religious activities, there was a Christian group upstairs with live music that bled down, and it made meditation more difficult. Even though the Buddhist group had met there for many years, the student leaders decided they wanted a quieter space, so they began to look. She went on to describe this scenario:

> That's why we've been kind of moving to different classrooms. And it's very interesting, wherever we go there's always music out there . . . . so it's challenging. And also, one other thing is that for us, for our meditation practice, we need cushions, right? When we were in Earl Hall, we had a space to put all the meditation cushions. But when we're moving to different classrooms, our student leaders, literally, they have to carry all these cushions. So, that's also very challenging.[68]

Just as the staffing of campus spiritual life has not been structured for the diverse demographics that are on campuses today, often sacred spaces have not been either, which presents challenges.

In addition, at some institutions, there have been tensions between secular mindfulness and meditation programs and religiously and culturally based Buddhist meditation programs. Some Buddhist chaplains, like The Reverend Doyeon Park have not seen this as much of an issue. She said,

> [At] both NYU and Columbia, they have different meditation or mindfulness practice. They're offered by different departments of the schools, right? Like wellness centers, they offer their own mindfulness practice. And there are so many, I see from flyers and programs, there are many different meditation or mindfulness

---

67. Doyeon Park, interview with author, November 17, 2020.
68. Doyeon Park, interview with author, November 17, 2020.

practices offered from the schools. I don't really see any kind of conflicts with them. As you said, because I see it's pretty clear.[69]

However, if secular meditation and mindfulness is all that is presented, it leaves out a great deal of the Buddhist tradition. Venerable Upali Sraman mentioned, for instance,

> By mindfulness, I don't just mean the breathing in and out technique. It's a very broad training mechanism for self-cultivation. So, it is just a key term, but then within it comes a great deal of techniques, methods, and disciplines for self-cultivation. I don't think all of that is being taken into consideration in places where people claim to practice mindfulness, but there is a lot more going on in the practice of mindfulness . . . If this wider scope is also brought into consideration and people actually practice them, it will be even a greater benefit.[70]

Part of a wider understanding of mindfulness in Buddhism also includes Buddhist ethics, which may not be given attention if meditation and mindfulness are divorced from their Buddhist roots. As Venerable Upali said,

> These kind of things are not popular knowledge, that Buddhism has a lot of insights that can be used for, for example, nowadays climate change is a major issue. So, bringing awareness about climate change . . . and even racism. So, in ancient India, Buddhism was one of the first, Buddhism and Jainism, they were the first few traditions, I think, globally who were challenging stigma around the birth of a person, all these discriminations. So, there is a lot of potential about bringing Buddhism into actual conversations about actual issues in the world.[71]

The challenge he said is that, "People idealize Buddhism because of mindfulness in many ways. So, this is what I mean, when you talk about mindfulness, it's not just about breathing techniques for emotional wellbeing. It's actually a very big, major ethical training system. So, climate change and racism, these are major issues now. And I think Buddhism can play key roles actually."[72]

---

69. Doyeon Park, interview with author, November 17, 2020.
70. Upali Sraman, interview with author, November 13, 2020.
71. Upali Sraman, interview with author, November 13, 2020.
72. Upali Sraman, interview with author, November 13, 2020.

Finally, an issue that has begun to arise more over time are tensions in the tradition over race and between birth-Buddhists and converts to the tradition. These are questions about the proper way to practice, even about what Buddhism is, and inclusivity. The Reverend Doyeon Park described,

> A lot of students that I work with at schools, they're all like, Americans. They're not actually those who came from Buddhist cultures. Well, lately, in the recent couple years, I have had more Chinese students and not many Korean students . . . . I have quite good Chinese students. Students from Taiwan are good. Like India, but the majority of the students are typical American kids who usually grew up with Christianity and are starting to discover Buddhist teachings.[73]

Asked about conflicts she said, "a couple years ago there was a little bit of conflict with the student leaders who were . . . [non-Asian] students, but they're so very sincere in the Buddhist practice. Then there are actually students from China, who literally had a lot of Chinese sutra-reading of their own Buddhist tradition in their home. Among those students, they had some conflicts. . . . " Asked how she handled it she said, "Well, I had a meeting with them one by one with the different students. And also when I talked to the Chinese students . . . . I think part of me because I also came from Asia, I kind of understand why they could think [in a certain way about the teachings]. But I offered, maybe you want to see some other aspects. So that well, they had seemingly pretty good . . . conversations for the last time before they graduated."[74]

The different ways that college Buddhists come to the tradition, along with their family and past experiences, can have an impact on their expectations. Park continued, "[Some students were] very strong, they had a very strong idea of what Buddhism should be like, what Buddhists are, if you are a Buddhist you have to follow certain practices or rituals, all these things. . . . In the Buddhist teaching, when we see it from the Buddhist perspective, there's no such thing that you should follow."[75] Park went on to say,

> In this case, I could be . . . very straightforward to these students, because I kind of understand that cultural aspect. So, I said, maybe that was your understanding before you come to the States. Now that we're here in the United States, we need to really see what

---

73. Doyeon Park, interview with author, November 17, 2020.
74. Doyeon Park, interview with author, November 17, 2020.
75. Doyeon Park, interview with author, November 17, 2020.

other religions are out there, what other people are kind of taking this teaching. And then also, if we really go deeper into the Buddhist teaching, would you say that the Buddha would have this perspective? Of course not, we recall Buddhist compassion.[76]

Buddhist chaplains can help to navigate some of these tensions that may arise, from the lived experiences of practitioners and the ways and the forms that Buddhism has come into their lives, and also ways that perhaps different forms of practice can exist in the same community, while also promoting anti-oppressive and anti-racist justice work.

For additional insight, I interviewed Lama Rod Owens, an authorized Tibetan Buddhist teacher, the author of *Love and Rage: The Path of Liberation Through Anger*,[77] and one of the founders of the Buddhism and Race Conference when he was a student at Harvard Divinity School.[78] He described how the history of how Buddhism became popular in the United States has in part caused the current racial dynamics in dharma communities: "Dharma [originally] came through Asian immigrants, through Chinese, Japanese, Korean immigrants, since the 1800s really. And then in the [19]60s and '70s, white folks started bringing it here because they were in India and Nepal and all over. So, it started coming here in a huge wave, and of course that was translated through white supremacist culture."[79] Some of this Buddhism that is filtered through white American culture is overly focused on meditation and mindfulness, rather than on community and justice issues:

> And so, you have a culture of dharma, mainstream dharma that's predominantly white and not really talking about justice because those weren't the values of practitioners. They just wanted to sit quietly and meditate and have transformative experiences in a meditation hall. And it wasn't about community either. It was about coming to the meditation hall, sitting quietly and doing meditation and leaving. And that was not how Asian and Asian-Americans created community and established community, and that's not how I understand community as well.[80]

---

76. Doyeon Park, interview with author, November 17, 2020.

77. Owens, *Love and Rage*.

78. Harvard Buddhist Community at HDS, "Third Annual Conference on Buddhism and Race."

79. Rod Owens, interview with author, November 17, 2020.

80. Rod Owens, interview with author, November 17, 2020.

Currently Black Buddhists, such as the contributors to the new volume, *Black and Buddhist: What Buddhism Can Teach Us about Race, Resilience, Transformation, and Freedom*,[81] are seeking to address these issues of inclusivity in American dharma communities, in which Buddhist concepts about the impermanence of the illusory world come up against the suffering caused by oppressive cultures and systems. At this point, Lama Rod says, he had decided not to try to reform the current system but rather to innovate: "I'm not like a reformist anymore. I'm more of an innovator. And when I say innovator, I mean I stepped outside of the system and just create new spaces instead of trying to reform old spaces. And that's so much of what we're trying to do in my community, is that we just wanted to start from the ground, starting from scratch and just building in values of inclusivity in everything that we do."[82] Building the values of inclusivity and justice into existing groups can be a challenge, although campus groups are increasingly taking that on—engaging in challenging conversations about dharma practice and racial justice.

Future

As Buddhism in America and American Buddhist communities are developing, so too is the emerging practice of Buddhist chaplaincy, which represents a changing and growing part of the Buddhist tradition and also of the field of chaplaincy. As The Venerable Upali Sraman said, "I totally agree with that idea that chaplaincy is also changing, and a lot of things are happening organically . . . and that's quite beautiful if we just see the pattern about how it is happening. I think it's really beautiful to see what is unfolding in front of us."[83] One thing that all of the Buddhist chaplains I interviewed have seen and experienced firsthand is the demanding nature of American higher education today, and how it can give rise to the suffering and stress that Buddhism is meant to address and alleviate, through aspects such as the technology of meditation. Kotatsu John Bailes describes today's college students in this way:

> [Many are] deeply habituated to be resistant to being present . . . Socially, we modern people are habituated to avoid discomfort

---

81. Yetunde and Giles, *Black and Buddhist*.
82. Rod Owens, interview with author, November 17, 2020.
83. Upali Sraman, interview with author, November 13, 2020.

completely. I think it's sort of a weakness. It's not like we have to suffer traumatically, but if we don't learn how to pay attention through some difficulty, not much can happen in our lives. I found that this [Buddhist chaplaincy] program as I began instituting it, helped students to get some access to their own, what I'll call subjectivity. [Our students] . . . they've all been competing and all been well-measured, and all have sized up what they have to know to get where they are in order to get to the next step and the next step after that. And if I don't have this in place now, how am I going to be an investment banker? Or when am I going to get into medical school? And so on.[84]

Part of what his program seeks to teach is how students can be present and at some peace in the midst of adversity. He went on,

But what I've found with [our] students . . . is they don't trust their own subjectivity. They may have their own opinions and so on, but they're always looking outside for reinforcement and measurement of who they are . . . to a third party expert, shall we say, which would be the person who gives them an A. As my first Zen teacher said to me when I was twenty, he said, 'This isn't about getting an A.' It took me a while to figure out what that meant, and I have my own version of that. So, in the course, all they need to do to get their PE credit for this course is show up and do some of the homework. [But] then they find it extremely difficult to sit still for 10 minutes, right?[85]

He said the goal is being present with discomfort through meditation and also taking the time to really cultivate their own subjectivity and reflect on their lives independently of external praise or blame. And yet while living and learning interdependently in a community where competition is not a value, students can develop their own integrity and their own spirit and values.[86] In Bailes' meditation courses, the students as a group,

experience that discomfort together. [It] softens them up and when they share about trying to do their homework of these different mindfulness exercises across the board, and they begin to see 'Oh, you're having difficulty, too. I'm not the only one. Oh, this works for you? Oh, that doesn't work for me, blah blah blah.' But they begin to relate on a horizontal level, and they begin to open

84. John Bailes, interview with author, November 23, 2020.
85. John Bailes, interview with author, November 23, 2020.
86. John Bailes, interview with author, November 23, 2020.

up and share in a way that I think they tend not to in your average seminar, because they're actually finding out that they're in a bit of uncharted territory, and they also find out this is interesting. So one student said to me, "You mean there's no way to know how well I'm doing? This is all my experience?" I said, "Yeah." ... She said, "I never knew I had a spiritual life until I took this course."[87]

All of the Buddhist chaplains spoke about the ways that meditation and mindfulness are currently growing on their campuses, which suggests that Buddhist chaplaincy could have a strong place in that, as a deeply spiritually and philosophically informed core of these offerings. The Reverend Doyeon Park said,

> So mindful NYU is actually getting really bigger at this current time that people are more interested in this contemplative kind of mindfulness practice.... They have different programs. And like at NYU, from the Mindful NYU team, they offer like, Monday to Thursday meditation programs. So, I am taking one of the nights like Tuesday evening, I lead the meditation, but other days they also have other teachers from other traditions.[88]

With that she said, Buddhist chaplaincy may also grow. However, as she said, "Well, because we're really like it's close to zero, it has to grow. Right? My friend who is a Won Buddhist teacher, ... maybe two years ago, she became the first Navy Buddhist chaplain. And now she's serving in some other countries ... So, I see different opportunities coming up."[89]

As Venerable Upali Sraman suggests, though, the growth of Buddhist chaplaincy in higher education will depend on university leaders and chaplains who understand the resources that these newer religions to the U.S. can offer in the higher education setting and then create positions. He said, "Maybe we need more people like [deans] who can connect these to the university, who have access to these students and who know the needs of these students. And also who know that there are things in Buddhism and Hinduism and other religions as well, that can benefit the university community."[90]

Indeed, the potential that a growing Buddhist chaplaincy has for higher education is not limited to Buddhism but would ideally include

87. John Bailes, interview with author, November 23, 2020.
88. Doyeon Park, interview with author, November 17, 2020.
89. Doyeon Park, interview with author, November 17, 2020.
90. Upali Sraman, interview with author, November 13, 2020.

Buddhism as a major world religious tradition. Some have suggested with the rise of those who may not claim a singular religious identity that these practices would lose interest, but that does not seem to be the case as The Reverend Doyeon Park said:

> I know people say in the future, less and less people will be interested in religions or spirituality. People are saying that there are going to be no religious people out there, and then all these religious institutions will kind of collapse . . . But . . . I think as long as there's a humankind . . . out there, [spiritualities will persist], because this is about what we are and how we live as a very genuine question of who we are. I personally think no matter what happens, there are going to be always people who are into this type of practice and who see the value of this kind of this practice and spirituality.[91]

Also, not only do Buddhist chaplaincies offer spiritual practices, but they offer a connection to the interfaith exchange needed for a diverse world, something needed here in the U.S. and abroad. She went on to say, "I think that's the kind of direction, we really need to create the space for students to see how we can actually live with people from different backgrounds . . . . Particularly I am very happy to see that schools are seeing the importance of this kind of . . . interreligious cooperation at school. . . . When I introduce what I do on campus to my friends back in Korea, because they don't really have such things there, they are kind of inspired to hear what we're doing in these places."[92]

Finally, it does seem that through the work of Buddhist chaplains and through broader interfaith work, awareness of the integrated and intersectional roles that chaplaincies can play is growing. As Kotatsu John Bailes said,

> Something has happened . . . since I've been at Wellesley, that more and more people across the community, and initially it was the division of student life, began realizing the central importance of the chaplains across the board in their work and then what assistance we could provide. And then slowly what's happening is a number of the academics in other parts of the institution are recognizing this . . . I think, in a different way. They need great help

---

91. Doyeon Park, interview with author, November 17, 2020.
92. Doyeon Park, interview with author, November 17, 2020.

> in reframing their old idea of what they think we do. They need it a great deal, and they need some experience of it.[93]

The Venerable Upali Sraman agreed, for all the reasons that have been discussed: "I think that most chaplains have a major role to play in the university through chaplaincy programs. So, I hope there are in the future more opportunities for Buddhist chaplains. And there is a need. I think maybe people didn't know that this was a need before, or they didn't recognize it."[94] Seeing the positive impacts of chaplaincy integrated into the institution, however, helps to reveal the need.

---

93. John Bailes, interview with author, November 23, 2020.
94. Upali Sraman, interview with author, November 13, 2020.

4

Humanist Chaplaincy

History

MOST PEOPLE SEE THE start of Humanist chaplaincy in American higher education beginning with Tom Ferrick (1929–2014), who served as Harvard University's Humanist chaplain from the 1970s to 2005.[1] As reported by his successor, Greg Epstein, the current Humanist chaplain at Harvard and MIT,[2] Ferrick grew up in Boston as an orphan after his parents died of tuberculosis, and he went to the College of the Holy Cross and then seminary to become a Catholic priest. He accepted a first assignment as a Catholic Chaplain at Dartmouth College, and while at Dartmouth, Ferrick's identity shifted in two significant ways—he stopped believing in God, and he realized that he was a gay man. This double revelation meant in his mind that he could not in good conscience continue serving as a Catholic priest. However, Ferrick remained deeply committed to moral development and to pastoral care, he got involved in the Ethical Culture movement founded by Felix Adler, and he moved to St. Louis, Missouri to become a leader in the Ethical Culture Society in St. Louis.

When a leader position opened at the Ethical Culture Society of Boston, Ferrick moved back to Boston, and he also connected with Harvard University and began serving as a Humanist chaplain. In the early years, his work there was supported by the Humanist and social philosopher Corliss Lamont, part of a prestigious family of Harvard alumni, who gave Ferrick

---

1. Marquand, "Thomas Ferrick, 84."
2. Greg Epstein, interview with author, November 24, 2020.

about $5000 per year in the early days.³ Later in 1995, an estate endowment given by John L. Loeb provided modest funds to support the programmatic initiatives of the Harvard Humanist chaplain.⁴ Ferrick was the first non-Christian or non-Jewish chaplain at Harvard, and the first nonreligious chaplain at any major U.S. university. Over the years, Ferrick continued his pastoral work on campus and in the community.

Around 2001, Greg Epstein, who had grown up Jewish and studied Chinese religions in college and lived in China, returned to the U.S. as a Humanist and wanted to continue into spiritual study and leadership. He enrolled for rabbinical ordination at the Institute for Secular Humanistic Judaism.⁵ Then on a visit to Boston, a mentor suggested that he meet Tom Ferrick, and it became clear that Ferrick, then in his mid-seventies, was considering retirement.⁶ Epstein then applied to Harvard Divinity School to pursue a Master of Theological Studies and he served as an assistant Humanist chaplain with Ferrick in 2004-2005, after which Ferrick stepped down and the Harvard Humanist Chaplaincy board appointed Epstein to be its next chaplain, as he completed his rabbinical ordination.⁷ Epstein brought to the Harvard Humanist Chaplaincy a vision of a new Humanist movement that he articulated in a conference honoring Ferrick for his 30 years of service at Harvard, and in a book he published in 2010 called, *Good Without God: What a Billion Nonreligious People Do Believe*.⁸

After serving as chaplain for a few years, Epstein decided to try to gather a Humanist congregation in Harvard Square which rented a space at 30 JFK Street and was called the Humanist Hub. The Hub opened on December 8, 2013, the same month that Ferrick died.⁹ As I witnessed from my position as the university chaplain at Tufts, for four and a half years until it closed on August 31, 2018, the Humanist Hub served as a well-known Humanist congregation, linked to but separate from the Harvard Humanist Chaplaincy. It attracted and mentored a circle of prominent Humanist leaders including Chris Stedman, who went on to become the first Humanist chaplain at Yale; Vanessa Zoltan, who with Casper ter Kuile developed

---

3. Greg Epstein, e-mail with author, March 21, 2021.
4. Arenson, "Alumnus Expands Love Affair with Harvard."
5. Greg Epstein, interview with author, November 24, 2020.
6. Greg Epstein, interview with author, November 24, 2020.
7. Byrne, "Humanist at Harvard."
8. Greg Epstein, interview with author, November 24, 2020.
9. Greg Epstein, interview with author, November 24, 2020.

the popular podcast "Harry Potter and the Sacred Text"; John Figdor, who became a Humanist advisor at Stanford and worked with Ideas Beyond Borders; and Walker Bristol, who became the first Humanist chaplain at Tufts University and later a hospital chaplain. The Harvard-MIT Humanist Chaplaincy also helped to form James Croft, who became the senior leader of the Ethical Culture Society in St. Louis, one of the largest Ethical Culture congregations, and Nina Lytton, an MIT alum who became a full-time UU Humanist hospital chaplain.[10]

During those years, the Humanist Hub offered Sunday gatherings, a children's education program, public lectures, service initiatives, and other events, which were quite popular, but which shifted the community's focus away from the Harvard Humanist Chaplaincy and the campus and also became hard to manage from a financial perspective. The costs of rent in Harvard Square, multiple staff salaries, and the program for such a congregation, even with the national attention it received, was unsustainable, and so the Humanist Hub closed in 2018. Since then, Epstein has continued to serve as the Humanist chaplain at Harvard and MIT, and to focus on his research, writing, and speaking.[11]

Chris Stedman, the one-time assistant chaplain at the Humanist Hub, was born in the twin cities of Minnesota and grew up in a secular household but converted to Evangelical Christianity at age eleven during his parents' divorce.[12] In college at Augsburg University, he struggled to reconcile his conservative Christian faith with his emerging gay identity, and he eventually became an atheist. Nevertheless, he remained interested in religion and decided to pursue a master's degree at Meadville Lombard Theological School in Chicago. While there, he began to work for Interfaith Youth Core, a Chicago-based nonprofit interfaith organization led by the Muslim American interfaith leader Eboo Patel, who introduced him to the Humanist movement by way of Greg Epstein's book. After theological school, Stedman applied to join the Harvard Humanist Chaplaincy and worked there as an assistant chaplain for several years, during which time he wrote his memoir, *Faithiest: How an Atheist Found Common Ground with the Religious*.[13][14]

---

10. Greg Epstein, email with author, March 21, 2021.
11. Greg Epstein, interview with author, November 24, 2020.
12. Chris Stedman, interview with author, November 20, 2020.
13. Stedman, *Faithiest*.
14. Chris Stedman, interview with author, November 20, 2020.

In 2014, Stedman was invited to become the coordinator of Humanist life at the Yale Humanist Community, a new independent nonprofit that was established to promote Humanism and Humanist community at Yale.[15] Stedman served that community for four years, before returning to Minnesota to become a fellow and an instructor in democracy and citizenship at his alma mater, Augsburg University.[16] Part of what Stedman has been known for, and sometimes criticized for by other atheists, is his embrace of work with religious people and of interfaith work, as he discussed in his memoir.[17]

As described by Tufts Humanist chaplain Walker Bristol,[18] during the years of the Humanist Hub, students at Tufts University in nearby Somerville and Medford, Massachusetts, who had a longstanding and active atheist and agnostic student organization called the Tufts Freethought Society, became involved in the Humanist Hub. They were a circle of students interested in regular intellectual conversations as well as campus activism on progressive causes such as LGBTQ nondiscrimination, sexual consent culture, labor rights, and environmental justice. The Tufts Freethought Society became increasingly interested in having a Humanist chaplaincy staff position at Tufts that would support them, and they explored the possibility of a Tufts Humanist chaplain through conversations with Humanist leaders like Epstein and Stedman, with Tufts alumni like Ellery Schempp, with Tufts faculty like Daniel Dennett, and with the university chaplaincy and administration. Initially a Humanist position did not make sense in the vision of the chaplaincy at the time, which had been more theocentric.

When I was appointed Tufts university chaplain in 2013, I met with the students interested in a Humanist chaplaincy including Walker Bristol, and I realized the potential value it could add to the broader interfaith work of the university chaplaincy and to making the chaplaincy accessible to more of the campus community. Revising the chaplaincy vision to center the search for spirituality, truth, and meaning as the chaplaincy's core purpose, we proposed to the office of the president that we add a position of Humanist in Residence as a part-time pilot paid staff position, and that became the first such institutionally-employed Humanist chaplain position

---

15. Chris Stedman, interview with author, November 20, 2020.
16. Chris Stedman, interview with author, November 20, 2020.
17. Stedman, *Faithiest*.
18. Walker Bristol, interview with author, November 24, 2020.

HUMANIST CHAPLAINCY

in the United States.[19] After Walker Bristol graduated from Tufts, they enrolled at Harvard Divinity School, and they were later hired as the first Tufts Humanist in Residence, a position that became their field education placement, and later grew to have the title of Humanist chaplain.

Bristol developed the Tufts Humanist Chaplaincy from initially providing support for the Tufts Freethought Society (which later became the Tufts Humanist Community) to eventually including a range of related programs and initiatives, such as work with the CARE office (on sexual consent), work with the LGBT center (on Transgender Day of Remembrance and other initiatives), work with the Veterinary School (on its Pet Loss Hotline), work on a Death Café (to facilitate student conversations about death and grief), as well as work with the university chaplaincy overall to help raise awareness about pastoral care. As a direct program of the Tufts university chaplaincy and a paid position, this role has remained one of the more stable Humanist chaplain positions nationally.

During recent years, several other Humanist chaplaincies in higher education have developed, mostly led by unpaid advisors. For a few years, Rutgers University has had such an affiliate, as did Stanford, the University of Southern California (USC), Columbia and NYU, and a few others.[20] In 2017, USC hired Vanessa Gomez Brake, a Humanist, as associate dean of religious life, and while her job is not to be a Humanist chaplain per se, she is believed to be the first Humanist hired into such a leadership role.[21]

Recently, several seminaries have explored the possibility of developing programs in Humanist chaplaincy, the first to do so being the University of Humanist Studies in the Netherlands, and many Humanists have also been affiliated with Harvard Divinity School, especially given its proximity to the Humanist Hub. The American Humanist Association has formalized a way for chaplains to be endorsed through the Humanist Society, which several Humanist chaplains recommended as an important credential.[22] Nevertheless, without robust support from the American Humanist Association, the Secular Students Alliance, or other such national bodies, potential Humanist chaplains and chaplaincies in higher education struggle to have the financial capacity to make a living and the professional resources to build a robust nationwide campus movement. Despite the

19. Stedman, "Tufts Creates First University-Funded Humanist position."
20. Humanist Chaplaincies, https://Humanistchaplaincies.org.
21. Silverman, "Humanist Chaplain Takes the Lead."
22. Humanist Society, "Humanist Chaplains."

growing numbers of entering university students who identify as atheist, agnostic, nonreligious, or spiritual but not religious at many research universities and other institutions, most institutions have not as yet decided to hire paid Humanist chaplains, and doing so as part of university religious and spiritual life remains controversial in some places. Even though much of organized Humanism has shifted from being anti-religious or secularizing to promoting the constructive values of Humanist ethics and partnering with religious people through interfaith work and social justice efforts, in some places, feelings of a deep divide remain, even in ways they do not seem to for other traditions that may be nontheistic, like Buddhism.

Preparation

Interestingly, perhaps because there is less of a traditional path toward professional Humanist chaplaincy than there is for any of the other traditions explored in this book, the Humanist chaplains I interviewed had many thoughts about the proper preparation for Humanist chaplaincy, and recommended more strongly some of the traditional elements of training for chaplaincy than chaplains of other historically underrepresented traditions in chaplaincy.[23] The preparation commonly seen as important included knowledge of the tradition (i.e., Humanist heritage, thought, worldview, and identity); knowledge of the "arts of ministry" (such as pastoral care); and knowledge of the higher education context. The Humanist chaplains I interviewed seemed to agree that the academic preparation usually acquired through a master's degree was important, as well as a form of endorsement or ordination, given that many in universities may not be familiar with Humanist chaplaincy and organizations. In addition, given that many Humanist chaplains will be developing their programs with no precedence, and that many exist outside of established structures, nonprofit management may be an important skill.[24] Interestingly, one chaplain suggested that having another side career would be valuable, since Humanist chaplaincy itself may not provide a sustainable living wage to support a family,[25] and another emphasized the importance of a candidate's identity being nonreligious—since some may see these roles as a kind of "multifaith chaplain," whereas the role is intended to create access to chaplaincy for

---

23. Chris Stedman, interview with author, November 20, 2020.
24. Walker Bristol, interview with author, November 24, 2020.
25. Greg Epstein, interview with author, November 24, 2020.

those who have historically been left out, namely the nonreligious.[26] All of the chaplains I interviewed emphasized the importance of multifaith religious literacy for being able to engage in interfaith work.

Of course, to be a Humanist chaplain, an initial prerequisite is a deep professional knowledge of Humanistic heritage, thought, worldview, and identity. Greg Epstein, who included an overview of Humanist history in his book *Good without God* said, "I think there needs to be some significant balance between training in Humanist thought and the heritage of Humanism . . . The intellectual aspects of Humanist work, and in chaplaincy of one way or another."[27] As Chris Stedman explained, this is important because, "just as, if you're becoming a Lutheran chaplain or a Lutheran pastor, you need to have some foundation in both chaplaincy and in Lutheran tradition . . . Because . . . mostly people come to Humanism at some point in their life but don't have any formal training in it, the history of Humanism as a worldview and an identity [is needed]."[28] Stedman, who has been serving as a thought partner and advisor with some institutions considering training programs in Humanist chaplaincy, went on to say, "I also didn't have a formal training in Humanism either. And that's why I'm very excited about this track that is developing . . . . That is about making sure that people who are studying to do Humanist chaplaincy can get the pastoral training they need and the Humanism as a worldview training."[29] This sort of training, a combination of heritage and thought in the tradition, as well as skills in ministry or leadership, are most often acquired through a Master of Divinity degree—but Humanists might not readily relate to that language. Stedman went on,

> I wish, if I could do it all over again, I had done an M.Div. I didn't enter into an M.Div. program because I didn't even know . . . I heard 'M.Div.,' and I thought, 'Well, that's obviously not for me.' And so, I did an MAR in pastoral care and counseling. And I found myself wishing I had had more training, more experience. I think I did the best I could under the circumstances. But I think I would have really benefited from having more training, from having ongoing training and professional support.[30]

26. Walker Bristol, interview with author, November 24, 2020.
27. Greg Epstein, interview with author, November 24, 2020.
28. Chris Stedman, interview with author, November 20, 2020.
29. Chris Stedman, interview with author, November 20, 2020.
30. Chris Stedman, interview with author, November 20, 2020.

Beyond the knowledge of Humanist heritage and thought, all of the Humanist chaplains I interviewed stressed the importance of training in various skills of chaplaincy, or what might be called the "arts of ministry" or spiritual leadership. Several stressed that pastoral care is essential. Walker Bristol said, "With the expectations of the role, I just think you do need counseling experience or some sort of indication that you're able to effectively and appropriately hold counseling relationships and intervene in those sorts of things."[31] This might be acquired through coursework such as Chris Stedman did at Meadville Lombard Theological School, or, as Greg Epstein said, potentially though a unit or more of Clinical Pastoral Education (CPE).[32] Among the arts of ministry, Bristol also stressed training in program development, since usually Humanist chaplains will be building their own programs from scratch. As Bristol said, "I think there is a very unique kind of program development. You're not going to have a lot just laid out in front of you. You do really have to kind of create. There's some aspect of it, I think, critically, about creating new programs that also are meeting . . . they're following what students want to do."[33] Even more so, they said, if the program will be a nonprofit, and living outside of Humanist or university structures—skills in nonprofit leadership and management may be important.[34]

Additionally, all of the Humanist chaplains I interviewed stressed the importance of knowledge of American campus contexts. As Epstein said, this may come, as in his case, from training as a rabbi and then interning in a campus setting, or from having another background in campus work.[35] Also, in keeping with his focus on connecting Humanists and the religious, Stedman stressed the importance of Humanist chaplains developing religious literacy, to be able to work with those of other worldviews:

> I also think that Humanist chaplains . . . need to have the things that all chaplains need to have, multifaith literacy . . . and especially given the fact that the students that chaplains are working with today are often coming into school with . . . a multifaith background, . . . or at least they've grown up in a multifaith community.[36]

31. Walker Bristol, interview with author, November 24, 2020.
32. Greg Epstein, interview with author, November 24, 2020.
33. Walker Bristol, interview with author, November 24, 2020.
34. Walker Bristol, interview with author, November 24, 2020.
35. Greg Epstein, interview with author, November 24, 2020.
36. Chris Stedman, interview with author, November 20, 2020.

Humanist Chaplaincy

In addition, all of the Humanist chaplains agreed that, given the unstructured nature of Humanist chaplaincy, some form of ordination or endorsement is useful for recognition, connection with mentors and peers, and support. Chris Stedman said, "When people reach out to me now and ask about Humanist chaplaincy . . . I almost always advise people to go through the UUA or the Ethical Society, because I do think that having that institutional support makes a huge difference in your experience of the work."[37] He said this is for a number of reasons, which he explained by saying:

> I think it's probably a little bit of everything, right? If you have this certification, it makes it a little easier for you to have access, to be recognized as legitimate in the work that you're doing. And I think for good reason, right? If anyone can just claim to be a Humanist chaplain, well, how is someone supposed to know whether or not they have the necessary qualifications or experiences? And so, I do think it's totally valid for institutions to say, "Well, who is this person?"[38]

The emphasis on obtaining a sort of certification for Humanist chaplains is for professional recognition and employability, and another benefit is for professional support. Stedman explains that:

> On an individual level, I also think that having that larger body that gives you support, that plugs you in . . . When you're doing chaplaincy, you're constantly hitting walls, obstacles, etc. And to have people who . . . [have] your back, ...You develop mentors, peers. You develop skills that you can draw on . . . I mean, all of these things that, I think, are so essential to doing this work.[39]

Walker Bristol was hesitant about professional accreditation when they first started, but now they think that it is important and valuable, whether from the UUA, the Ethical Society, the Society for Humanistic Judaism, or the American Humanist Association. They said,

> Part of it is because of the celebrancy [license], the way that it allows you to be a celebrant. But part of that is also there is some role accountability. And they're growing a lot more resources for chaplains specifically. [The Humanist Society] was really geared towards celebrants for many years, and now they're starting to

---

37. Chris Stedman, interview with author, November 20, 2020.
38. Chris Stedman, interview with author, November 20, 2020.
39. Chris Stedman, interview with author, November 20, 2020.

say, 'we have a lot more chaplains, let's do more stuff for chaplains ... And I think that, with a dearth of professional organizational structure for even just chaplains, I think that that is valuable.[40]

In addition, Greg Epstein stressed that, given that Humanist chaplaincies are currently not well supported financially either by Humanist organizations or by most universities, having another career can be very important for personal and family livelihood. While earlier on he imagined that one day there would be many Humanist chaplain positions, now Epstein recommends that, " [Humanist chaplains have] some other way of moving through the world and ultimately making a living—whether it's that you're an entrepreneur, filmmaker, a lawyer, a social worker, a therapist, something . . . " On the one hand, this is because currently Humanist chaplaincy is not lucrative itself, and people entering this field should have some financial stability, "because on a practical level, you got to have some kind of career." But also, Epstein believes, having another kind of expertise, whether as a vocation or an avocation, is part of the human thriving that Humanism promotes for all, "because I think it's consistent with Humanism in a way. There's a belief that you can only be human through a certain prism and you have to choose a prism, and become something of an expert at looking at the world through that prism."[41] In Epstein's view, having a career or significant avocation is a part of the idea of developing a meaningful life as a Humanist person.

Finally, and interestingly, Walker Bristol emphasized that it is important to remember that Humanist chaplain positions are not only intended to be general chaplaincy positions but are intended to provide some representation and access for the nonreligious, and therefore Humanist chaplains should ideally identify as nonreligious. They explained:

> I think that I know lots of people who describe themselves as Humanists with a little 'h,' . . . and who care a lot about justice and accessibility, but who are Christians or they're religious or they're religious in a certain way and that's a priority for them... I'm just saying, because of how the term itself doesn't have, it can be used in different ways, I think that it might attract an applicant pool of people who would say, 'Yeah, I'm a Humanist in some ways, but I have a lot of roots in this tradition and stuff.[42]

40. Walker Bristol, interview with author, November 24, 2020.
41. Greg Epstein, interview with author, November 24, 2020.
42. Walker Bristol, interview with author, November 24, 2020.

Bristol, who comes from a Quaker background personally, sees the role of the Humanist chaplain as really to make a space for the nonreligious. They went on, "It's very, very important to me just in terms of what I bring to the role and not necessarily a requirement, to say, well, I serve an important role on this team and for this university that I make our space a lot more accessible, or communicate that our space is accessible, to people who are not religious or not religious in a traditional way."[43]

Whereas in other cases where it might be clearer when a tradition-specific chaplain is serving their own community and when they are serving the community more broadly, for Humanists it is less clear. Bristol said, "I do think that it's important to have an eye towards, to remember, the reason we have this position is in part to be able to provide these resources and programming and be attentive to a particular subset of our community, and I worry sometimes that that might get lost if the door is open without that explication of like, . . . it's not just a little 'h' Humanist chaplain."[44]

Responsibilities

As with most chaplaincy in higher education, all of the chaplaincies of the Humanist chaplains I spoke with were centered on a student organization and its community and activities. Ryan Bell, the volunteer Humanist advisor at USC, said that his normal schedule on campus was about eight hours per week.[45] This would generally involve weekly lunch on Wednesdays at a vegan café, and a Sunday night dinner cooked by the associate dean of religious life's husband who is a chef. At USC, the organization is called the Secular Students Fellowship, and Bell says their "bread and butter" is big intellectual and philosophical discussions, about such things as the ethics of Artificial Intelligence, death and dying, etc. Each year there are different student leaders, some of whom have more vision and energy for the group and it evolves with what they want it to be.[46] According to Bell, prior to his tenure, Bart Campolo served as the Humanist advisor, and he had specific ideas about student programming and implemented the Sunday suppers as potlucks, to be a non-threatening way for students to bring their friends and just have low-key social time enjoying hospitality.

---

43. Walker Bristol, interview with author, November 24, 2020.
44. Walker Bristol, interview with author, November 24, 2020.
45. Ryan Bell, interview with author, November 23, 2020.
46. Ryan Bell, interview with author, November 23, 2020.

Bell has other ideas of things he would like to implement, such as to help build a Humanist community for faculty and staff, or to offer a course such as Introduction to Humanism, or start a lecture series open to the public.[47] As a volunteer though, the time he has available for USC is limited, given his full-time job at the Secular Students Alliance, a national nonprofit that supports 300 student-led secular groups, and his other work on tenants' rights and housing justice. Bell would also come to campus when there were tragedies, however, such as the attacks on the Tree of Life Synagogue and the Christchurch Mosque, when he would participate in campus vigils.[48] Another part of being an affiliate he said was participating in monthly religious life affiliate meetings with USC's office of religious life, that included an educational component for religious life affiliates about campus life, on topics such as mental health services or a campus addiction recovery house.

At Harvard and MIT, Greg Epstein spoke of seeking to create a similar culture with the Harvard Community of Humanists, Atheists, and Agnostics (HCAA). He said, "I think a lot of discussion programs work really well, small group discussions where you ask people to tell you what's going on in their lives and what's going badly in their lives again and again and again on a regular basis, work really well. And I would do those again every time I could."[49] Earlier on, he said he sought to impose more of a vision of what the group should do. He said, "The thing that . . . I really regret not understanding in the previous years, is that I'm a chaplain for these students that are under so much academic and other kinds of pressure, and I would never, in this era of my life and career, I would never do some of the stuff that I used to do, where I would put pressure on the students to put on extensive programming."[50] Now, Epstein sees his role as to support the students and encourage them to thrive together: "I would say go out and be activists together, make films together, podcasts together. Make music together. Just hang out and have deep philosophical, pretentious parties together. Sit around and have retreats and talk about what kind of human beings we want to be, what life we want to live. And be easygoing about it."[51]

47. Ryan Bell, interview with author, November 23, 2020.

48. Ryan Bell, interview with author, November 23, 2020.

49. Greg Epstein, interview with author, November 24, 2020.

50. Greg Epstein, interview with author, November 24, 2020; Greg Epstein, email with author, March 21, 2021.

51. Greg Epstein, interview with author, November 24, 2020.

Humanist Chaplaincy

One thing in particular the Humanist Hub used to do, that Epstein fully supported at the time and does not regret supporting, but that he no longer supports his organization doing because he has become philosophically opposed to it, is charitable service projects such as meal-packing for people experiencing food insecurity. On that topic, he said:

> I'd be really concerned now, that programs like that as a chaplaincy initiative, really reify the idea that the answer to people not having good food to eat is to put dry food in boxes and give it to them for free as a charity handout. . . . I want to be part of something that breaks that . . . about our society and rebuilds it better. Because I just don't want to endorse in any way, tacitly, this idea that there should be so many people who just don't have healthy food to eat.[52]

Epstein has become more interested in activism to address the root causes of systemic social issues such as food insecurity, housing insecurity, etc. He wants Humanism to be "the place that you can take refuge in where you understand that it's all about just being a human being, caring about other human beings, caring about how you live your life, supporting people, recognizing biases that we face and the prejudices that we face."[53]

Epstein also added that he thinks interfaith dialogue and engagement, being present for interfaith dialogue and interfaith work of various kinds, is a major Humanist imperative.[54] This is very much in the tradition of Tom Ferrick, who as the first non-Christian or non-Jewish chaplain at Harvard worked hard to support the diversity, equity, and inclusion of all religious and philosophical groups at the university. Epstein thinks that being part of interfaith work is one of the most important things for Humanists to do, and that more Humanists will engage in interfaith work in the future. While in the past, some secular Humanists would be opposed to working with the religious and would think that what was most important is "right beliefs" about scientific questions, Epstein suggests that what is most important is "right actions" for good in the world with others.[55]
He said:

> [What is critical is one] being willing to step forward and say, 'Here's who I am. Here's what I believe. I make no compromises

---

52. Greg Epstein, interview with author, November 24, 2020; Greg Epstein, email with author, March 21, 2021.

53. Greg Epstein, interview with author, November 24, 2020.

54. Greg Epstein, interview with author, November 24, 2020.

55. Greg Epstein, interview with author, November 24, 2020.

about what I personally believe. However, I also recognize that the things that I believe are not necessarily all one needs, or enough to be a good human being. I'm a good human being because I'm part of a society of different people who have different beliefs, who I can learn from, who I must learn from. Tell me what you think, as part of the inclusive society that you're trying to build.[56]

Chris Stedman said that at Yale, what he was doing as a Humanist chaplain,

> was very similar to what Harvard does, what Tufts has done.... I do think we did some pretty cool things at Yale. But I do think that they all fell into that category that, I think, most Humanist chaplaincy functions as, which is, let's look at how religious communities are trying to meet these needs for their populations. And let's try and create a Humanist version of that, which is more of a top-down approach rather than a bottom-up approach of saying, 'What are the needs of this population? And what are particular things we can develop that will meet those needs?'[57]

Recently Stedman has been spending more time thinking about those questions of needs-assessment for nonreligious people. But meanwhile, his chaplaincy energies have moved into a different medium, in the classroom, teaching an Augsburg University religion and philosophy course on "The Search for Meaning."[58] He said that class bears similarities to the discussions he led as a Humanist chaplain, although they take place in a class: "My job in teaching that class is to help them think through what their sense of vocation is, where they find meaning in their lives, what their story is, all these things that I was trying to do as a chaplain. So, when I was first asked to teach this class, or invited to teach this class, I was like, 'I'm not qualified.' But I've since come to realize it's very much the work I had been doing."[59] And, as has been a common activity of his and Epstein's, he has been continuing to write and speak publicly. His new book, *IRL: Finding Realness, Meaning, and Belonging in Our Digital Lives*,[60] is about, "what the search for meaning looks like in this digital moment, when more and more people are leaving the traditional institutions . . . and are moving that work to digital

---

56. Greg Epstein, interview with author, November 24, 2020.
57. Chris Stedman, interview with author, November 20, 2020.
58. Chris Stedman, interview with author, November 20, 2020.
59. Chris Stedman, interview with author, November 20, 2020.
60. Stedman, *IRL*.

space, . . . turning to the internet for a sense of belonging, a sense of identity, a sense of meaning."[61] So he says he feels that he has been continuing to extend similar ideas and work, though not in chaplaincy per se.

At Tufts, Walker Bristol began by leading a small group reflection program that was more facilitated, a bit different from the discussion meetings that the Tufts Freethought Society had previously offered. But Bristol's work quickly expanded into other areas that probably would not have been possible for the student organization to do alone, such as confidential one-on-one support counseling, or pastoral care. Bristol's accessibility for pastoral care built on work they had done as a trained rape crisis counselor with the Boston Area Rape Crisis Center (BARCC), and it quickly expanded among students who valued this type of "check in with a chaplain," as the students reported they generally call it.[62]

Over the 2019–2020 academic year, Bristol and some of their colleagues in the Tufts university chaplaincy conducted an internal review to learn more about pastoral care practices in the Tufts university chaplaincy team, and also to survey 40–50 students who had made use of the pastoral care services of the office to learn about their experiences.[63] The review explored some of the history of pastoral care in higher education, what the best practices are from peer institutions, how pastoral care is defined, how it is publicized to students, how it is explained to faculty and staff, whether there should be more of a system for referring students based on various chaplains' areas of expertise, relationships with other university offices like the counseling center, the professional development chaplains may want to have about pastoral care, etc.[64] This process itself also provided the opportunity for the staff to communicate with each other about pastoral care, and to create more intentional awareness about this quieter but nevertheless highly valued aspect of chaplaincy work.

Bristol also learned that to build a Humanist chaplaincy required doing outreach by going to where the nonreligious students were and seeing how to be of support. As they said,

> If one third or so of students, now about 40% or so of students at Tufts, would say they're not religious in one way or another across the undergraduate and graduate schools, we weren't having 3,000

---

61. Chris Stedman, interview with author, November 20, 2020.
62. Walker Bristol, interview with author, November 24, 2020.
63. Walker Bristol, interview with author, November 24, 2020.
64. Walker Bristol, interview with author, November 24, 2020.

people at Freethought meetings, obviously, right? . . . But those people are still making meaning, those people are still asking similar questions to what a chaplaincy might offer, they're still doing lots of those things. And what became, what also became clear, early on in the role, was the need to enter into, to meet people where they are. To go into other communities, and not just in general, for a general principle of being accessible, but because, really, that was where nonreligious meaning making was happening in a lot of ways.[65]

As Bristol was aware, this nonreligious meaning-making was happening in the CARE office, in the LGBT center, in campus social justice work, etc. As Bristol described, "It was happening in other places where people were like, ' . . . I have Humanist principles, I don't need to go to a Humanist community, I need to go out and protest, I need to go out and live out my values in another way.'"[66] Therefore the Humanist chaplaincy began to develop intersectionally with other campus spaces where nonreligious students were—in the School of Veterinary Medicine which had a high percentage of nonreligious students who cared about veterinary issues and emotional health; in the CARE office where students were wrestling with issues of sexual misconduct, sexual health, and sexual and consent education; and in the LGBT Center, where, as a non-binary person and a Humanist, Bristol felt there could be more attention drawn to the human dignity of transgender people killed each year by transphobic violence.[67]

Bristol also created a program that lifted up Humanist voices from other sectors, such as hospital and military chaplaincy, and brought to Tufts a popular program called the Death Café, that invited students to think together about death and grief, which are often taboo topics.[68] As a developmental issue that arises frequently for college students, Bristol realized a first significant loss can be a spiritual and emotional crisis for students, and if they are nonreligious or do not believe in an afterlife, they may not have access to the traditional spaces and rituals for making sense of their loss and grief. As they said, such programs may not be ones that students would naturally identify as things they would want to do by themselves, but

---

65. Walker Bristol, interview with author, November 24, 2020.
66. Walker Bristol, interview with author, November 24, 2020.
67. Walker Bristol, interview with author, November 24, 2020.
68. Walker Bristol, interview with author, November 24, 2020.

their popularity has shown that they do fulfill a need that students have, for making meaning when they may not do so religiously.[69]

Challenges

There are several facts about Humanism itself as a tradition that make the development of Humanist chaplaincy in higher education more challenging. Not only, as with some other historically underrepresented traditions in chaplaincy, is chaplaincy new to the Humanist tradition, but also many atheists, agnostics, nonreligious, and spiritual but not religious people may not relate to the term "Humanism" itself. "Humanism" has emerged as an umbrella term to describe atheists, agnostics, nonreligious, and spiritual but not religious people in more positive and proactive terms. In the words of the American Humanist Association, it represents "a progressive philosophy of life that, without theism or other supernatural beliefs, affirms our ability and responsibility to lead ethical lives of personal fulfillment that aspire to the greater good."[70] Other definitions speak of Humanism as "a rational philosophy informed by science, inspired by art, and motivated by compassion."[71] It affirms the dignity of every human being and supports the maximization of individual liberty and responsibility, advancing democracy, human rights, social justice, the appreciation of nature and culture, science, love, happiness, creativity, and service.[72]

Nevertheless, many who may hold these values and whose worldview may fall into the categories described as "Humanist" may not themselves use the term or even recognize it upon arriving at college. As Ryan Bell said,

> The main thing that comes to mind right away is that people don't recognize Humanism as a thing. It certainly doesn't have the name recognition that the major religions of the world have. Atheism is not really, to me, a good organizing principle. . . . You could be a fascist and be an atheist. . . . There's nothing special, in my view, about being an atheist. I don't put that badge on my shirt.[73]

---

69. Walker Bristol, interview with author, November 24, 2020.
70. American Humanist Association, "Definition of Humanism."
71. American Humanist Association, "Definition of Humanism."
72. American Humanist Association, "Definition of Humanism."
73. Ryan Bell, interview with author, November 23, 2020.

Developing and constructing an identity based on what one does not believe may not be attractive as an organizing force or something that people feel the need to bond over. Bell continued, "I am an atheist, and it's interesting to talk about sometimes, or whatever, if you want to get into the philosophy and theology of that, which I do enjoy, but practically speaking, it's not a very good organizing principle. It's sometimes challenging."[74] All of the Humanist chaplains I interviewed talked about the idea that this might be a kind of "marketing challenge"—people not recognizing the name "Humanism" or knowing why they would want to associate around something they are not (i.e., believers), or something that seems self-evident to them. Bell went on to say,

> It's almost so self-evident to some people that it doesn't seem like a thing. It's like, our value system is based on human agency, and that humans are responsible for their lives, the lives of others, and the planet, and that we believe that, in as much as our problems can be solved, it lies with us to solve them. People go, like, 'Oh, yeah. That makes sense, but I'm not going to go to church for that.' … You know?'[75]

So, in addition to not necessarily using the label "Humanism," those with Humanist beliefs may not associate with chaplains or know why they would connect with an office of religious life. Even if they might be dealing with some of the challenges Humanist chaplaincy seeks to address, such as the desire for caring community, or for philosophical conversation, or to put their values into action in the world, it might require education for people to know that that is what Humanist chaplaincy is and can be.

Several of the Humanist chaplains admitted that another challenge of Humanist chaplaincy might not just be recognition, branding, or education, but the fact that many Humanists themselves might not actually be seeking a Humanistic version of traditional religious life. On the one hand, some of the elements of spiritual community that Humanists have developed have been attractive to some, such as those who were historically attracted to the Ethical Culture movement, people who attended the Humanist Hub, and even Humanistic Unitarian Universalists, Jews, or Buddhists. As Ryan Bell said,

---

74. Ryan Bell, interview with author, November 23, 2020.
75. Ryan Bell, interview with author, November 23, 2020.

I think we're always wrestling with, do we do the kind of church knockoff where we do Humanist church? Which a lot of people love, and there are those, of course. . . . They all do the same things. They have a guest musician. They might sing some songs, corporately, together. They'll usually have a reading, or a poem, or some kind of scripture, if you will, and then a sermon, and then some announcements . . . You know? It's a model that is time-tested. On a campus, I don't think that's so much the vision as it is to say, "How can we be a resource to students? An intellectual, moral kind of guidance, a resource . . ."[76]

Bell noted how there is an epidemic of loneliness on college campuses, many students struggle to fit in, and therapy is not really the only answer to having caring community.[77] But Chris Stedman wonders whether the nonreligious are really seeking Humanistic community. He said, "I think one of those assumptions is that people who have either left or were never part of a religious institution are looking for something that, in some way, functions like a religious institution does. And I'm just not sure that that's true."[78] Having worked in Humanist community building for most of a decade, when he left Yale to return to Minnesota, local Humanist groups asked if Stedman would work on Humanist community-building there. But he decided that a better approach would be to do a needs assessment among the nonreligious there and to see what they would want.[79] So he has been working with sociologists at the University of Massachusetts Boston and the University of Minnesota to develop a survey that takes this more community-organizing approach. He has been asking the questions of young nonreligious people like, "What does community actually mean to you? What do you expect to get from it? What do you expect to give to it? Where are you currently finding community right now? What kinds of practices are you doing to help make sense of your lives?"[80]

Stedman senses that, "even as the number of nones are growing . . . it's largely these 'nothing-in-particulars.' And my sense is that, for them, they are not really looking for a formal space that's structured around making sense of their lives in the way that religious spaces do. I think . . . they don't expect to find a sense of community or identity in being a Humanist

76. Ryan Bell, interview with author, November 23, 2020.
77. Ryan Bell, interview with author, November 23, 2020.
78. Chris Stedman, interview with author, November 20, 2020.
79. Chris Stedman, interview with author, November 20, 2020.
80. Chris Stedman, interview with author, November 20, 2020.

and being nonreligious."[81] He thinks that for this generation, it may be that thinking about beliefs and values, if it happens, will happen in more formal settings like the moral philosophy course he is teaching, which could be likened to the capstone courses for undergraduate seniors that university presidents used to teach.

In addition, those who have attempted to build Humanist chaplaincies and congregations, even at highly visible, well-resourced, and seemingly receptive institutions have found it very difficult to do so sustainably, due to lack of Humanist organization support and lack of university financial support. As has been mentioned, there is currently no national Humanist organization to serve as a "sending body" for Humanist campus ministers to university campuses. While the American Humanist Association will endorse Humanist chaplains through the Humanist Society, the endorsement does not currently involve the kind of deeper sponsorship, mentoring, and support that religious denominations' licensing and ordination processes offer. The American Humanist Association also does not fund chaplains, and so whatever chaplaincies develop are either the result of local nonprofit organizing, such as at Harvard and Yale, or direct university support, such as at Tufts. As Chris Stedman said of his work at Yale,

> There isn't a body that . . . supports Humanist chaplains right now. I was also just doing it very much on my own. I didn't really have any institutional support. So, ultimately, it wasn't sustainable. It wasn't possible to keep doing it. . . . And I think it's really meaningful and valuable. I also think it's very difficult right now to do that work that is as demanding as that work is, without the institutional support that it needs and that it currently rarely has.[82]

Both Stedman and Greg Epstein discussed the work of trying to build a congregation or community that requires regularly working twelve-hour days and trying to do something like six jobs in one, from leading the nonprofit, to program leadership, to pastoral care, to community organizing, to communications, to fundraising. As both of them shared separately, trying to do all of that singlehandedly without extensive external support took a great toll.[83][84]

---

81. Chris Stedman, interview with author, November 20, 2020.
82. Chris Stedman, interview with author, November 20, 2020.
83. Chris Stedman, interview with author, November 20, 2020.
84. Greg Epstein, interview with author, November 24, 2020.

Humanist Chaplaincy

At the current time, making a concerted effort to invest in college and university chaplaincy has not been a priority of national Humanist organizations, which have traditionally been more focused on issues such as the separation of church and state, legal work, awareness-raising, publications, conferences, and some courses.[85] The Secular Students Alliance has become more interested in advancing a positive Humanism on campuses, that connects with issues such as Black Lives Matter, but it does not have the resources to pay or place chaplains.[86] And while colleges and universities that track their religious and philosophical identification data may be aware of the growing numbers of students who might fit within the Humanist category on their campuses, most have not moved in the direction of allocating funding to create Humanist chaplaincies that would center and specifically serve these students. According to all the Humanist chaplains I interviewed, the work is certainly there to do if there were funding. As Ryan Bell said, with funding from the institution, higher education's resources for Humanism are vast:

> Then funding, I think, is a huge challenge. If I were there full time, every day, I could do all kinds of stuff, it'd just be great. Resources are not the problem. You just have endless resources. From the professors that are on campus who are Humanist-adjacent, whether it's philosophy, history, science, you name it. Then, online resources, and physical spaces. The campus is a mecca of physical spaces, libraries . . . . The whole place is a secular temple.[87]

Finally, although the Humanist chaplains I interviewed were reluctant to name it as "prejudice" or "discrimination," there are ways in which Humanism and Humanist students, faculty, and staff have tended to be treated with at least "systematic negligence" that has prevented their interests and needs from being centered in university spiritual life programs, despite the fact that their numbers are quickly approaching the majority on many campuses. Walker Bristol recalled the critical press that conservative websites published when the Humanist chaplaincy was becoming established.[88][89]

Bristol also described some of the ways that, in their other work as a hospital chaplain, they have seen a kind of discrimination against

---

85. Chris Stedman, interview with author, November 20, 2020.
86. Ryan Bell, interview with author, November 23, 2020.
87. Ryan Bell, interview with author, November 23, 2020.
88. Stanford, "Tufts Puts 'Humanist' Chaplain on Its Own Payroll."
89. Morrongiello, "First of Its Kind."

Humanism function, especially in the context of other identities and communities where religious belief and belonging might be presumed.[90] While many colleges and universities have been regarded as safer spaces for Humanists and "secular temples," Ryan Bell shared that biases against atheists, agnostics, and the nonreligious can still persist, and persist even in the idea that Humanists do not need or want the resource of chaplaincy.[91] In addition, since many Humanist organizations have long been predominantly white, male, and upper-class, the spaces and resources available to support Humanists who might be people of color, women or transgender, and/or working class are fewer.

Future

By the numbers, now should be a time for Humanist chaplaincy to be on the rise, given that according to recent data from the Pew Research Institute, the number of Americans with no religious affiliation continues to rise significantly, along with a sharp drop in the percentage of Americans identifying as Christian.[92] Over the past ten years, the number of Americans identifying as Christian has dropped from 77% to 65%, while the number of Americans identifying as atheist, agnostic, or nonreligious has risen from 17% to 26%.[93] The percentage of Protestants is down from 51% to 43%, and the number of Catholics is down from 23% to 20%.[94] Significantly, there is a wide age gap as well, with 75% of baby boomers identifying as Christian and only 49% of millennials.[95] Given these continued rapid changes in the American religious landscape, and especially in the steep changes among young adults, with the numbers of people who might be described in the broad category of Humanism growing, it would seem Humanist chaplaincy would be a relevant resource for a growing number of college and university students.

In some ways, by definition, Humanist chaplaincy has been on the growing edge of chaplaincy, and that is both a challenge and an element that makes it intriguing and exciting. Walker Bristol, who for several years

90. Walker Bristol, interview with author, November 24, 2020.
91. Ryan Bell, interview with author, November 23, 2020.
92. Crary, "Number of Americans with No Religious Affiliation."
93. Crary, "Number of Americans with No Religious Affiliation."
94. Crary, "No Religious Affiliation."
95. Crary, "No Religious Affiliation."

convened a series called "New Directions in Chaplaincy" as part of the Tufts Humanist Chaplaincy, said that the uncharted, experimental, and cutting-edge nature of Humanist chaplaincy is part of what made it exciting for them:

> And, so, that was . . . what kept me there for now seven years . . . . in some ways, the lack of a model I was expected to fit into, for that role. And I think my colleagues from minority traditions maybe feel . . . but I've heard similar things, that those challenges can either be very deflating or they can be very exciting, the challenges of not having that model, not having the steppingstone if you're a non-Christian chaplain. And I think that I experienced both, but I certainly experienced the energizing piece enough to continue to do it.[96]

While it can certainly be a challenge that the work of Humanist chaplaincy is uncharted territory, it seems based on current demographics that Humanist chaplaincies are seeking to serve a rising tide or a growing trend in young adult spiritual life. In that sense, while Humanist chaplaincies have the challenge of not being able to rely on an established tradition, they are also therefore a space for creativity. This seems to be ever more often the case, as many Humanist groups seem to be changing from having an anti-religious or skeptical focus and being generally more interested in intellectual discussion, to having a positive focus on proactively advancing Humanistic values, such as holistic wellness, the creative arts, interfaith engagement, and social justice.

Also, as much as the need or desire for Humanist congregations or communities might seem to be in question, it does seem as though interest in Humanist chaplaincy and caregiving persists. All of the Humanist chaplains I interviewed expressed that they regularly hear from young people interested in getting involved in Humanist chaplaincy, either as chaplains or as participants. Greg Epstein said,

> I think that fortunately people have now recognized that there's a need for this sort of thing, at a much greater level. And there are more people interested in it. I mean, I just talked yesterday to a 23-year-old . . . where this person just had decided while they were at college, that what they really, really want to do with their life is to become a Humanist chaplain. And I get a few of those every year, every single year, it used to be once a month. But now

---

96. Walker Bristol, interview with author, November 24, 2020.

it's still like once every couple of months that I get one of those. So, the people are into it. The population as we know very well is getting much less religious and people are searching for new ways to make meaning and connect to community and understand their values.[97]

Walker Bristol said, "It's hard to say what the future is, but I don't experience the future as, it's not deflating, I guess. So many more students are interested in talking to me; every year it's more people wanting to talk to me, every year, new students want to be involved. We were worried this year [during the COVID19 pandemic], 'Oh, gosh, is no one going to want to come to our remote meetings?' I think we have more people coming to [our] meetings than any other religious student group, honestly . . . "[98]

Additionally, Chris Stedman also said he feels that Humanist chaplaincy is important and he is invested in its development and future success, having served as a thought partner with institutions considering training programs in Humanist chaplaincy.[99] Still though, he encourages those interested to be realistic about the challenges of the work and to seek to connect themselves with structures and communities for their support.[100] Walker Bristol suggested that even if Humanist congregations and communities may not take hold, there is still an important role for Humanist chaplaincy. They said,

> Humanism is changing, and maybe Humanist communities aren't exactly the way of the future—they may not be what the world looks like . . . a bunch of Humanist communities in ten years. [But] it may still be the case where we have a lot of Humanist chaplains because they offer something really important to what a chaplaincy is doing on a college campus, and they communicate something very important to the college campus about who the chaplaincy is for."[101]

In short, they help to open up the chaplaincy for the changing demographics—for the many students, faculty, staff, alumni and families who are nonreligious.

---

97. Greg Epstein, interview with author, November 24, 2020.
98. Walker Bristol, interview with author, November 24, 2020.
99. Chris Stedman, email with author, March 21, 2021.
100. Chris Stedman, interview with author, November 20, 2020.
101. Walker Bristol, interview with author, November 24, 2020.

Humanist Chaplaincy

Given that one of the main challenges for Humanist chaplaincy is funding, the Humanist chaplains I interviewed suggested a number of ways that this challenge might be overcome in the future. Greg Epstein shared a number of ideas that he thinks could make it work financially, although he said "none of them is in any way guaranteed."[102] One would be a generous donor: "An individual could come along who got really enamored with the idea and create a lot of money to support it. A few million bucks would make a big difference. Spent the right way . . . Whether by investing in training at the divinity school level, or creating a few modest part-time endowments to go along with some other work or whatever," such as Harvard's Loeb Humanist endowment. A related possibility would be estate gifts: "It could be that with some older Humanists dying . . . that they decide to put their will towards this."[103]

Another possibility would be that national Humanist organizations could take on supporting university and college chaplaincies as a priority and an investment in the future. Epstein doubts that will take hold, but Ryan Bell sees it as an important priority, for Humanists who care about a future for Humanism:

> I think Humanists really need to invest in the next generation. Conservatives in this country really get that. . . . They're nurturing those people, getting them into their orgs, flying them to D.C., all expenses paid. Introducing them to this world where their eyes get big and they say, 'Wow. This is something. I could really be a power player in this world.'[104]

As some of the other chaplains from historically-underrepresented traditions gestured toward, he said: "I'm not saying we have to appeal to the baser instincts of people, [such as that Humanist values are under attack] necessarily, but I think we could be nurturing people from a younger age with an eye to raising up people of significant, important values to be leaders in our country, in our society, in business, and every other area. I think trying to build a foundation or a monetary foundation for chaplaincy."[105]

And the other possibility would be for more universities and colleges to take on this responsibility and designate the funds, as part of their support for diversity, equity, and inclusion goals. As Epstein said, "It could

---

102. Greg Epstein, interview with author, November 24, 2020.
103. Greg Epstein, interview with author, November 24, 2020.
104. Ryan Bell, interview with author, November 23, 2020.
105. Ryan Bell, interview with author, November 23, 2020.

become more like Muslim chaplaincy where more and more universities and colleges are recognizing that they need to step up and fund the Muslim chaplaincy, because to say that they've got a chaplain's office and that they don't have a Muslim chaplain is no longer acceptable. So that's certainly something that you could see."[106] Along the same lines, Bell said,

> The other approach, I guess, would be to try to convince universities, one-by-one, that this is a significant and growing percentage of their student body, 40, up to 45% these days, maybe soon, the majority. If you're not really looking after the spiritual, so to say, needs of that group . . . , then that's a big piece of student development that's being left out. To think about funding Humanist chaplaincy from a university level, [some] private schools are doing it, where they don't have the fear factor of separation of church and state.[107]

This would require university chaplains and other university leaders advocating for this from a diversity standpoint. As Bristol said,

> You know, if I'm in leadership, in an environment like that, I might say, 'You know, we could really communicate something important to our community by creating this role that could really drive us to be the office we want to be, [serving all students]' . . . . And it's one of those kind of leadership decisions I think where you're sort of like, 'Well, I might not have a petition list of student names who would use this that I can bring to leadership or I can fundraise for, but I do have a strong instinct or I have a vision for how this would serve our community,' if that makes sense. It definitely makes a big statement about inclusion . . . to have someone with the title.[108]

Another possibility several of the Humanist chaplains I interviewed mentioned is that all chaplaincies might move into more of a Humanist direction. Chris Stedman said,

> If I had to take a wild speculation about the future of chaplaincy with very little grounding in any data, it would be that more and more . . . chaplaincies are going to move in the direction of [a kind of Humanist approach]. I think that a lot of small liberal arts colleges are already there in the sense that the chaplaincy has to be a catch-all for lots of people . . . . And it's not about watering down or

---

106. Greg Epstein, interview with author, November 24, 2020.
107. Ryan Bell, interview with author, November 23, 2020.
108. Walker Bristol, interview with author, November 24, 2020.

universalizing. But it's about saying that this is a space for reflecting on your values, on what gives your life meaning, opportunities to serve, to be in conversation.[109]

He cites as an example of a type of program that might relate to the religious, spiritual, and Humanistic alike, the kinds of "This I Believe" series that allows everyone to talk about what gives their lives meaning. Stedman described, "They do this thing every week where it's like a dinner. People can come for food. And every week, someone from campus talks about what matters to them. And so, one week, it's the university president. The next week, it's someone on the custodial staff. The next week, it's an administrative assistant in the department of biology. And it's truly people from all over campus."[110]

Whether it is through the term Humanism or other terms like "interfaith" or "spiritual," these Humanist chaplains see chaplaincies seeking to adjust to the changing demographics of their campus populations where people may be nonreligious, spiritual but not religious, hold multiple religious identities, or be exploring. Stedman has noted a trend in which some young adults seem less likely to connect to any fixed identity labels, of "discrete categories with rigid boundaries," and may rather be seeking "being a part of a web of people who are talking about identity and meaning in these various ways."[111]

While Bristol expressed the value of making chaplaincies explicitly hospitable to atheists, agnostics, the nonreligious, spiritual, and Humanist by using those terms, they also affirmed that discerning how to do that is experimental. They said,

> I see a lot of growth there, I don't know that I see that growth in the structure of university chaplaincies, but I do hear a lot more interest among, . . . I also know more people who their title is 'interfaith chaplain,' I hear that title more, I hear more people who are in that role that is a little bit less specific in religious life, but who have a lot of investment in their Humanist communities of students or their nonreligious communities of students. So, it's not that nothing's happening and things are dissolving, it's just I think we are all kind of bouncing back and forth on our feet to be able to

---

109. Chris Stedman, interview with author, November 20, 2020.
110. Chris Stedman, interview with author, November 20, 2020.
111. Chris Stedman, interview with author, November 20, 2020.

meet the needs of this rapidly changing landscape, and, really, it's changing rapidly.[112]

At one university, a trend of student deaths and suicides raised the question of the depression and anxiety many students seem to be feeling, arguably in part from students lacking the feeling of a caring community and the kinds of connection that religious communities and other voluntary associations once helped to provide.[113] In this context, Ryan Bell and others believe the kind of care and community Humanistic chaplaincy can provide could be part of the solution: "Students are in crisis, even at prestigious universities where they feel under so much pressure, and without a support system. Everyone knows the need, and I think Humanist chaplaincy isn't the only answer to the problem, but I think it's an answer. It's one piece of the puzzle to be in conversation with."[114]

He said, "these kinds of programs, in combination with religious offerings, Humanist offerings. I think, student affairs has been about this, like recognizing the whole person, and you're educating the whole person."[115] Humanistic chaplaincy is one place to develop where that happens. As Bristol said, this is less about putting out a sign and saying, "atheists and agnostics and Humanists come here," which may be working less and less for any particular community these days. The work of Humanist and other chaplaincy now is to get out, build bridges, and support people in making meaning and living out their values where they are, asking questions like, "What are you doing now? What are you doing around the election? What are you doing around COVID19? What are you doing around these things?"[116] The potential challenge of that, as Ryan Bell and others shared, is that it can lack the organized and collective power to advocate that congregations offer. As a former pastor, Bell says, "I think just the problem with Humanism being unorganized, as it often is, is that we're all just individuals floating around in the world with some really stellar values, perhaps, but no real mechanism by which to put those values into action in the world."[117]

One thing is clear, according to Humanist chaplains, that in order for Humanism to live up to its own principles, it needs to refocus on the

112. Walker Bristol, interview with author, November 24, 2020.
113. Ryan Bell, interview with author, November 23, 2020.
114. Ryan Bell, interview with author, November 23, 2020.
115. Ryan Bell, interview with author, November 23, 2020.
116. Walker Bristol, interview with author, November 24, 2020.
117. Ryan Bell, interview with author, November 23, 2020.

needs of those who have been peripheral in its movement—young people, women, and people of color—and it needs to center itself on justice issues, and people's material concerns. Greg Epstein discussed the irony of Humanism's foundational beliefs being a faith in and a love of humanity, and yet the organized movement in America has been mostly white.[118] And that has been a key question, as young Humanists especially have explored Humanist associations and found them to be largely older, white, and male. Ryan Bell offered a similar observation, "I'm running into the word 'Humanist' more and more. I find that different people mean different things by it. Especially if it's coming from a historical context, I think it's been very white, upwardly mobile, sort of Enlightenment tradition, which I think, especially in our current culture, is seen as very colonial and not really immediately . . . accessible to people of color. You could probably say that about lots of religions, being fairly prescribed in their audience."[119]

However, Epstein, Bell, and others see themselves as wanting to help build a corrective to that, a Humanist movement that Epstein describes as "diverse, inclusive, and inspiring," and that lifts up and centers historically underheard voices.[120] Both Epstein and Bell agree that this means Humanism must increasingly address "the material conditions of people."[121] Bell says, "I was making that argument when I was a Christian, and I think it just makes even more sense as a Humanist. I think Humanists have, by and large, shied away from taking positions or stands on economic issues that are sort of, broadly, [the] American capitalist kind of milieu."[122] He and others like Stedman have said some of the key concerns of some Humanists have been issues like the separation of church and state, rather than, for instance, Medicare for all. Bell went on, "If you ask me, when you think about maximizing the conditions for human thriving, which would be a way of talking about the goal of Humanism, how do you talk about maximizing the conditions for human thriving, without talking about the things that are standing in the way of people thriving? Which is like police brutality, minimum wage, healthcare reform, all of that stuff."[123]

---

118. Greg Epstein, interview with author, November 24, 2020.
119. Ryan Bell, interview with author, November 23, 2020.
120. Greg Epstein, interview with author, November 24, 2020.
121. Greg Epstein, interview with author, November 24, 2020.
122. Ryan Bell, interview with author, November 23, 2020.
123. Ryan Bell, interview with author, November 23, 2020.

Bell believes that thinking about Humanist community, or spiritual community in general, as about wellbeing, or making people feel better misses the point. It should rather be about making individuals and society be better—that is, about being more just. "Not to take anything away from the ecstatic experiences," he said, "I think those are also amazing, and wonderful. We all go to the movies, and read novels, and drink wine, if we drink wine, for all those reasons. An amazing meal, a great relationship. Those are all things that make us feel better, and hopefully, make us actually better in some cases."[124] But our Humanist movements that have come down to the present, he says, have "a legacy that has to be dealt with" to be putting their values into action. Of course, he says, there are systemic connections between issues like the separation of church and state, and progressive social issues such as fair wages, education, healthcare, and justice system reform.[125] He admires the work of leaders like Dr. Sikivu Hutchinson, who has been on the Los Angeles Human Relations Commission. Bell says,

> She's been an educator, a secondary educator, at a high school in South Central.... She has a scholarship program she runs through an organization called Black Skeptics of Los Angeles. She's a very outspoken atheist. She does not bend on her atheist bonafides, and her political, racial, class analysis is just sharp as a knife...."[126][127]

Bell says that recently the AHA has been seeking to change, "They have a Latinx Alliance. They have a Black Humanist Alliance. They have an LGBTQ+ Alliance. They're really trying to open the conversation to these other communities." Bell also notes that there is an organization now called Black Nonbelievers, a chapter-based organization, with about a dozen chapters around the country that holds a national conference once a year.[128]

Epstein has come to the realization, though, as he says the older Humanists tried to tell him early on, but he was not listening, that "Humanism is politics and politics is Humanism."[129] He says that while earlier Humanism supported Civil Rights, he believes it did not give race enough significance—attending to the ways in which American society has been founded on Indigenous, Black, POC, and other kinds of oppression. In order for

124. Ryan Bell, interview with author, November 23, 2020.
125. Ryan Bell, interview with author, November 23, 2020.
126. Ryan Bell, interview with author, November 23, 2020.
127. Molina, "Black Skeptics Find Meaning."
128. Ryan Bell, interview with author, November 23, 2020.
129. Greg Epstein, interview with author, November 24, 2020.

HUMANIST CHAPLAINCY

Humanism to truly embody and promote its own beliefs and values today, and to engage the next generation, politics must be central.[130]

For further insight, I reached out to Vanessa Gomez Brake who serves as an associate dean of religious life at USC.[131] Although her role is not to be a Humanist chaplain per se, she is herself a Humanist and has navigated both the challenges facing Humanists getting into chaplaincy work and also the challenges within some organized Humanist communities. Brake's own path into chaplaincy after her master of divinity was through working as an events specialist in the Stanford University office of religious life, which was an expansive role that included duties such as coordinating chapel programming, authorizing campus religious professionals and organizations, and supporting students both in the day to day and in crises. From her own experience, she spoke about the challenges facing Humanists to be regarded as legitimate in some university and religious contexts and how those have been compounded as a young woman of color. She said,

> I still am not considered legitimate by a lot of folks, whether people tell me that overtly or in the way they relate to me, but this is a question because I'm also a young woman of color. It's hard to piece it out you know, if I'm all these intersecting identities. I don't know what people are reacting to, I just know I've seen it regularly . . . and it's probably the reason I didn't use the Humanist label publicly for a long time just because whether it's negative perceptions about atheists and things like that or it's just the complicated question of "what is Humanism?"[132]

Brake spoke about how this question of the legitimacy of Humanism, compounded by dynamics of age, gender, and race, has also manifested in challenges for Humanists getting into the field of chaplaincy and embracing spirituality in higher education as a path. Although she did decide to continue her undergraduate studies of religion into seminary, she thinks many Humanists would imagine that seminary is not for them, and indeed the curricula at many seminaries are not adapted to focus on current Humanist concerns. Instead, she learned much about chaplaincy through women chaplain mentors:

> I was raised Catholic, and most often I couldn't see myself in a role of leadership because it just was drilled in my head that men are

---

130. Greg Epstein, interview with author, November 24, 2020.
131. Vanessa Gomez Brake, interview with author, February 25, 2021.
132. Vanessa Gomez Brake, interview with author, February 25, 2021.

leaders and women do something else. But a woman rabbi taught me how to read the Bible, and just having women in leadership helped me understand that leadership can take different forms.[133]

Such interfaith connections not only illuminated a path into leadership for her, but they have also influenced her as she has shaped a kind of Humanism that is more inclusive around gender and racial identities. Brake said such diversity has been less of an issue with the Humanist student communities she has worked with which have been diverse, but many of the organized Humanist communities she explored were more predominantly white and male and not as relevant to her own experience and concerns.[134] She spoke about personally joining a "secular sangha" that is made up of Buddhists and Christians, bound together by meditation, that meets in Little Tokyo in Los Angeles:

> It's made-up of a variety of Asian Americans, and so I'm seeing myself reflected in this group, and I'm also seeing people who themselves are seeking and not necessarily binding it to Christianity or Buddhism, even though they're informed by those traditions. They're open in a way that I feel like Humanist circles are not . . . I think a lot of people in the sangha are more generally open to new ideas or different expressions of understanding what is sacred.[135]

Brake spoke about what has been limiting in some Humanist circles in terms of both the topics that are discussed and the forms the meetings take, which can impact who feels welcome and who wants to participate. In many organized Humanist groups historically, she said, the topics of discussion have tended to focus on anti-religious sentiments and the format has often been lecture-style, with less openness to practices like ritual, or attention to the building of community.[136] She remembered one meeting in which a woman mentioned that she practices homeopathy, which others called out as being unscientific.[137] And for herself as well, coming from a Filipino background,

---

133. Vanessa Gomez Brake, interview with author, February 25, 2021.
134. Vanessa Gomez Brake, interview with author, February 25, 2021.
135. Vanessa Gomez Brake, interview with author, February 25, 2021.
136. Vanessa Gomez Brake, interview with author, February 25, 2021.
137. Vanessa Gomez Brake, interview with author, February 25, 2021.

> I had all sorts of folk religion, I guess you'd call it our Indigenous traditions, that we have in the Philippines, and we never called that "religion" because it was just a part of our way of life, part of our culture, and so forth, but as I got older I was just like, no, actually that's bound to certain things that provide us meaning like connection with our ancestors and connection with the natural world.[138]

Whereas in some Humanist circles, people might say those who practice such cultural traditions are not Humanist, she affirms an "expansive Humanism" that welcomes different ways of being Humanist and understands there can be as many varieties of Humanism as there are in other traditions. In the secular sangha she has joined and in the Humanist student organizations she has advised, Humanism might take the form of philosophical discussions, but it might also take the form of sharing vegan meals, meditation, service work, and open conversations about what is meaningful in life.[139]

Brake discussed how such an expansive view is shaping the overall religious life offerings at USC, which seek to "go where the student energy is going." USC Religious Life has moved away from traditional religious language in many cases because it is not familiar to many students and using it can filter them out in advance. She said,

> We talk about belonging, we talk about connection, we talk about life's big questions, all of that, and in that way, we're not saying we're specialists in religion and spirituality, but we're specialists in navigating this life experience, and so that's for everyone, our work is for everyone, and I want every student to have a sense that, whether they're religious, spiritual or not, that there is something for them coming out of our office.[140]

Whether through Mindful USC, "What Matters to Me and Why," programs designed to cultivate friendships, drumming circles, or "SoulJourns" to Los Angeles spiritual centers, for Brake and the Humanist chaplains I interviewed, the future of Humanist chaplaincy may look like the future of higher education chaplaincy broadly—seeking to make spiritual practices, interfaith learning, the cultivation of community, and reflective action

---

138. Vanessa Gomez Brake, interview with author, February 25, 2021.
139. Vanessa Gomez Brake, interview with author, February 25, 2021.
140. Vanessa Gomez Brake, interview with author, February 25, 2021.

more accessible to all.[141] Some would be critical that such approaches do not provide the richness that immersion in any one religious tradition would offer, or underscore the risks of cultural appropriation in separating spiritual practices from their complete contexts. But while traditional forms of chaplaincy rooted in particular forms of religious prayer, worship, scripture study, holidays, and other practices will certainly continue, for the growing numbers of students who do not identify with a religious tradition, such expansive humanistic chaplaincy programs may provide an entryway.

---

141. Vanessa Gomez Brake, interview with author, February 25, 2021.

5

Conclusion

THIS BOOK HAS EXPLORED the development of higher education chaplaincy in the United States in traditions beyond Christianity and Judaism over the past thirty years. Through interviews with chaplains serving in these roles—many of them the first in their institutions' histories—it has explored the stories of how these chaplaincy positions and programs have come to be, the background the chaplains had that led to their appointments, the shape of the programs they have developed, the challenges they have faced, and their perceptions of the future opportunities of higher education chaplaincies in their traditions.

The colleagues I interviewed revealed that the development of these chaplaincies has followed the growing religious and philosophical diversity of the United States, especially since 1965, as researched by Professor Diana Eck and the Harvard Pluralism Project.[1] These chaplaincies began to emerge as critical numbers of students from non-Christian and non-Jewish traditions reached American higher education. They developed in keeping with the dynamics described by theorists of religious life in higher education such as Douglas and Rhonda Jacobsen, who have indicated the influences of multiculturalism, globalization, and postmodernism on the revival and expansion of American higher education spiritual and religious life in recent years.[2]

In general, these developments have emerged from student interest along with administrative responsiveness and leadership as the key factors

---

1. Eck, *A New Religious America*.
2. Jacobsen and Jacobsen, *No Longer Invisible*.

in the diversification of college chaplaincy. Also decisive was the watershed moment of September 11, 2001, which revealed for many the religious and philosophical diversity that had been growing on college and university campuses in America, and the vast religious illiteracy that made the presence of these traditions and the interests and needs of their communities previously unknown to many who had historically been on campus.[3]

The events of September 11, 2001 and their aftermath called upon universities to both better serve and support their more diverse religious and philosophical populations, and to do more in the way of building religious literacy, mutual understanding, respect, and engagement, such as has been advocated by Boston University Professor Stephen Prothero[4] and by Eboo Patel.[5] This has led to an increase in the formation of university interfaith councils and interfaith programs that deepen awareness and that seek to build solidarity among those of all traditions and none in order to advance the common good and meet today's national and global challenges. However, the growth of chaplaincies along diverse lines has been slow at times, given several factors within diverse religious communities in higher education, which on the one hand may not have actively advocated for these resources, and on the other may not have led in providing them.[6] Some exceptions would be the models put in place at Wellesley College in 1993, and its resonances at institutions described in this book such as Howard, Brown, Princeton, Yale, Georgetown, Columbia, NYU, USC, Tufts, and Emory.

As these positions and programs have developed, more has become clear about the type of preparation candidates need to have to be optimally successful in these roles. Common to most is a grounding in their traditions personally and theoretically, knowledge of the "arts of ministry" such as spiritual program development, community organizing, and pastoral care, and a familiarity with the American higher education context. Depending on the setting and the structure, other skills such as nonprofit management may be needed.[7] In some cases, traditional religious education and formation is very valuable, but it often seems it needs to be coupled with a master's degree, ordination, or other credentialing in order to be

3. Omer Bajwa, interview with author, November 24, 2020.
4. Prothero, *Religious Literacy*.
5. Patel, *Acts of Faith*.
6. Vineet Chander, interview with author, November 20, 2020.
7. Celene Ibrahim, interview with author, November 23, 2020.

CONCLUSION

fully recognized and respected within the U.S. higher education system.[8] Professional associations for these newer fields in chaplaincy are developing as more standardization is sought in the field. Even just in 2020, the North American Hindu Chaplains Association (NAHCA) formed and held its first conference, and a research project is currently underway to map Buddhist chaplaincies in the U.S. A Muslim chaplains' Association is more well-established, and Humanist chaplaincy professional associations are still being explored and developed.

The programs among these chaplaincies vary somewhat, but core elements include: weekly gatherings, educational programs, pastoral care provision, service and social justice projects, interfaith work, and holiday and fellowship events. Some communities have also needed to focus on specific accommodation needs such as for sacred spaces, which often do not exist on historic campuses for traditions other than Christianity and Judaism. Muslim prayer spaces and ablution rooms are often added first, followed by space and equipment for Buddhist meditation and Hindu puja, and often interfaith spaces for use by all where communities can gather for learning, celebration, and solidarity. Other important accommodations center on halal and other religiously sensitive food, academic accommodation for holiday observances, and occasionally special needs regarding housing. Beyond addressing specific accommodations for individual communities, attention to issues of campus climate by addressing religious literacy and interfaith engagement for all students, faculty, and staff helps to build hospitable and anti-oppressive campus cultures. That is one reason why so many of these underrepresented communities are highly engaged in interfaith dialogue and action.[9]

Challenges these new chaplaincies face mirror the challenges these religious and philosophical traditions have experienced in the broader United States society, such as lack of recognition, lack of funding, lack of established support structures and networks, and the need to adapt and find footing in a space often alienating or even discriminatory toward these traditions and not established to include them. Chaplaincy itself is a new concept in all of these traditions, and in the case of Humanism, the intended population itself does not always even identify with the tradition's name.[10] Like other higher education diversity, equity, and inclusion work,

---

8. Vrajvihari Sharan, interview with author, November 20, 2020.
9. Omer Bajwa, interview with author, November 24, 2020.
10. Ryan Bell, interview with author, November 23, 2020.

this work involves transforming institutions that have competing priorities and can be slow to change, and so partnerships between interested students and institutional leaders with a vision and resources are needed.[11]

Looking to the future, the religious demographics of the United States seem to indicate that the diversification of college and university chaplaincy along the lines discussed in this study will continue to be valuable as American higher education seeks to serve its changing demographics and all students. Institutions are currently exploring best practices for how to lead in this area, as well as the questions this may raise for how to do higher education spiritual life overall, including for established communities. Work such as the Alexander and Helen Astin and Jennifer Lindholm's *Cultivating the Spirit: How College Can Enhance Students' Inner Lives*[12] indicates that this work is part of the soul of American higher education, and trends in the mental health and wellbeing of students among other measures seem to indicate that practices of spirituality and cultivating caring community continue to be needed. But creativity will also be needed to continue to adapt the university's resources and interventions to its changing demographics.

This book contributes to the literature of religious diversity in the United States and religion in American higher education by documenting some of the cutting-edge ways in which religious life on university campuses has been growing and changing over the past thirty years. It begins to fill a gap in the literature about some of this growth by recording and documenting some of this work being done by its practitioners. It was necessarily limited in scope in that it did not undertake to interview every practitioner of Muslim, Hindu, Buddhist, and Humanist chaplaincy in the U.S., but rather a sampling of leaders of exemplary programs representing diverse backgrounds in terms of gender, race, sexual orientation, geographic region, immigrant status, birth or convert status, and type of academic institution. Further research could take each of the traditions explored individually as a focus of study and could also examine more systematically the reception and impact these chaplaincies have had in their institutions over time, cutting into the data in different ways such as by exploring student, faculty,

11. Omer Bajwa, interview with author, November 24, 2020.
12. Astin et al., *Cultivating the Spirit*.

Conclusion

staff, and alumni impressions. As this is an emerging and growing field, there is much still left to study. However, I believe this book reveals that the work of chaplains of these several traditions has deep value and impact in responding to the changing religious demographics of the United States and serving our spiritually diverse communities.

※

This book has been written during the pandemic of COVID-19 and an ever-growing awareness of endemic racial injustice in the United States, and there are many ways in which the integrative work of spiritual and ethical life in American higher education beyond the classroom can be engaged on these and other pressing social issues on both individual and social levels. This study has informed my own efforts in leadership, which has been the calling of my career, from my student days at Brown and Harvard, to work at UC Davis, Oberlin College, Tufts University, and now Emory University, to expand the circle of diversity, equity, inclusion, and community in higher education spiritual life to welcome and support all students, faculty, and staff, and especially those who have been historically marginalized and underrepresented.

The process of writing this book has been valuable to me already as a university chaplain and dean of religious life who is engaged in deepening a university chaplaincy as a multifaith university chaplaincy team. Knowing more about the histories, the preparation, the responsibilities, the challenges, and the opportunities experienced by chaplains of traditions being added to multifaith teams has assisted me in my leadership—as I learned more about whom we might recruit for these roles and how we could shape these programs. I hope that it will also be helpful to university leaders and colleagues across the country who are similarly seeking to respond to the growing religious and philosophical diversity of their university communities with the appropriate resources to address the spiritual and ethical needs of their communities today.

I am deeply grateful to the chaplains who have mentored me, especially Janet Cooper Nelson and Peter J. Gomes, and to all those I interviewed and included in this study for their innovative work and for teaching me and all of us in a way that I hope will benefit them and other practitioners of these diverse traditions and our collective interfaith endeavors for spiritual growth and global thriving. These chaplains inspire me by their work, even as we are all continually inspired and blessed by the students, faculty, staff, alumni, families, and wider communities that the work of university chaplaincy gives us the great privilege to serve.

Appendix I. Interviewees

Name	Position	Interview Date

Islam

Name	Position	Interview Date
Omer Bajwa	Muslim Chaplain, Yale University	11/24/20
Celene Ibrahim	Former Muslim Chaplain, Tufts University	11/23/20
Nisa Muhammad	Assistant Dean of the Chapel, Howard University	11/11/20

Hinduism

Name	Position	Interview Date
Vineet Chander	Coordinator of Hindu Life, Princeton University	11/20/20
Vrajvihari Sharan	Director for Dharmic Life, Georgetown University	11/20/20
Asha Shipman	Director of Hindu Life, Yale University	11/15/20

Buddhism

Name	Position	Interview Date
John Bailes	Buddhist Chaplain, Wellesley College	11/23/20
Rod Owens	Activist and Author	11/17/20
Doyeon Park	Buddhist Advisor, Columbia and NYU	11/17/20
Upali Sraman	Former Buddhist Chaplain, Tufts University	11/13/20

Humanism

Name	Position	Interview Date
Ryan Bell	Humanist Advisor, U. of Southern California	11/23/20
Vanessa Gomez Brake	Associate Dean of Religious Life, USC	02/25/21

Appendix I. Interviewees

Walker Bristol	Former Humanist Chaplain, Tufts University	11/24/20
Greg Epstein	Humanist Chaplain, Harvard and MIT	11/24/20
Chris Stedman	Former Humanist Chaplain Harvard, Yale	11/20/20

About the Author

Gregory W. McGonigle is the dean of religious life and university chaplain of Emory University in Atlanta, Georgia, where he has built a multifaith chaplaincy team and has opened the Emory Interfaith Center. He has served in higher education chaplaincy for nearly twenty years at the University of California at Davis, Oberlin College, Tufts University, and Emory University, developing multifaith programs and supporting religious inclusion. He has also worked in congregational, legal advocacy, healthcare, and public health settings. He holds a bachelor's degree with highest distinction in religious studies from Brown University, a master of divinity degree from Harvard University, and a doctorate in ministry from Boston University. He is an ordained Unitarian Universalist minister and has served as a researcher for the Harvard Pluralism Project. He is past president of the National Association of College and University Chaplains and he has taught and mentored divinity students from the Pacific School of Religion, Harvard Divinity School, and Candler School of Theology.

Eboo Patel is the Founder and President of Interfaith America, a Chicago-based organization that is building the interfaith movement. He is the author of "Acts of Faith: The Story of an American Muslim, the Struggle for the Soul of a Generation" (Beacon Press, 2010), "Sacred Ground: Pluralism, Prejudice, and the Promise of America" (Beacon Press, 2012), "Interfaith Leadership: A Primer" (Beacon Press, 2016), "Out of Many Faiths: Religious Diversity and the American Promise" (Princeton University Press, 2019), and "We Need to Build: Fieldnotes for a Diverse Democracy" (Beacon Press, 2022).

Bibliography

Adams, Maurianne, et al. *Teaching for Diversity and Social Justice*. 2nd ed. New York: Routledge, 2007.
Ali, Muhammad A., et al., eds. *Mantle of Mercy: Islamic Chaplaincy in North America*. West Conshohocken, PA: Templeton, 2022.
American Humanist Association. "Definition of Humanism." https://americanhumanist.org/what-is-humanism/definition-of-humanism.
Angelakis, Constanos. "Humanist Chaplaincy, Freethought Society Discuss Future at Tufts." *Tufts Daily*, February 16, 2016.
Arenson, Karen. "Alumnus Expands Love Affair with Harvard by Offering a Monumental Gift," *New York Times*, March 15, 1995. https://www.nytimes.com/1995/03/15/us/alumnus-expands-love-affair-with-harvard-by-offering-a-monumental-gift.html.
Association of Muslim Chaplains. https://associationofmuslimchaplains.org.
Astin, Alexander W., et al. *Cultivating the Spirit: How College Can Enhance Students' Inner Lives*. San Francisco: Jossey-Bass, 2010.
Brown University. "Rumee Ahmed Appointed Brown University's First Muslim Chaplain." Aug 1, 2006. https://www.brown.edu/campus-life/spiritual-life/chaplains/news/2006-08/rumee-ahmed-appointed-brown-universitys-first-muslim-chaplain.
"Buddhist Ministry Initiative." Harvard Divinity School. https://hds.harvard.edu/academics/buddhist-ministry-initiative.
Byrne, Lauren. "Humanist at Harvard." *Harvard Magazine*, May-June 2005. https://harvardmagazine.com/2005/05/Humanist-at-harvard.html.
Cadge, Wendy. *Chaplaincy and Spiritual Care in the Twenty-First Century*. Charlotte: University of North Carolina Press, 2022.
Chander, Vineet. "A Room with a View: Accommodating Hindu Religious Practice on a College Campus." *Journal of College and Character* 14.2 (2013) 105–16.
Chander, Vineet, and Lucinda Mosher, eds. *Hindu Approaches to Spiritual Care*. London: Jessica Kingsley, 2019.
Chaplaincy Innovation Lab. "Hindu Chaplaincy in U.S. Higher Education." http://chaplaincyinnovation.org/projects/hindu-chaplaincy-higher-ed.
Convergence on Campus. "Announcing the North American Hindu Chaplaincy Conference." *World Hindu News*, May 10, 2020. https://www.worldhindunews.com/announcing-the-north-american-hindu-chaplaincy-conference/.
Crary, David. "Number of Americans with No Religious Affiliation Growing." *PBS News Hour*, Oct 17, 2019. https://www.pbs.org/newshour/nation/number-of-americans-with-no-religious-affiliation-growing.

Bibliography

Crosby, Pam. "Victor Kazanjian in the Heart of the Action: Persons of Purpose in the Profession." https://characterclearinghouse.fsu.edu/article/victor-kazanjian-heart-action-persons-purpose-profession.

Eck, Diana. *A New Religious America: How a "Christian Country" Has Become the World's Most Religiously Diverse Nation*. San Francisco: Harper, 2002.

———. *Encountering God: A Spiritual Journey from Bozeman to Banares*. Boston: Beacon Press, 2003.

———. "What Is Pluralism?" The Pluralism Project. http://pluralism.org/what-is-pluralism.

Ellison, Koshin Paley, and Matt Weingast, eds. *Awake at the Bedside Contemplative Teachings on Palliative and End-of-Life Care*. Somerville, MA: Wisdom Publications, 2016.

Ennis, Ariel. *Teaching Religious Literacy: A Guide to Religious and Spiritual Diversity in Higher Education*. New York: Routledge, 2017.

Epstein, Greg. *Good without God: What a Billion Nonreligious People Do Believe*. New York: HarperCollins, 2009.

Fields, Rick. *How the Swans Came to the Lake: A Narrative History of Buddhism in America*. Shambhala, 1992.

Forster-Smith, Lucy, ed. *College and University Chaplaincy in the 21st Century: A Multifaith Look at the Practice of Ministry on Campuses across America*. Woodstock, VT: Skylight Paths, 2013.

———. *Crossing Thresholds: The Making and Remaking of a 21st-Century College Chaplain*. Eugene, OR: Cascade, 2015.

Georgetown University. "Former Army Chaplain Now Heads Hindu Ministry at Georgetown." Oct 6, 2014. https://www.georgetown.edu/news/former-army-chaplain-now-heads-hindu-ministry-at-georgetown.

Georgetown University Office of Campus Ministry. "Georgetown Appoints First Director for Hindu Life and First Hindu Priest Chaplain in United States." Aug 8, 2016. https://blogs.commons.georgetown.edu/campusministry/2016/08/08/georgetown-appoints-first-hindu-chaplain/.

Goodman, Kathleen M., et al. *Educating about Religious Diversity and Interfaith Engagement: A Handbook for Student Affairs*. Sterling, VA: Stylus Publishing, 2019.

Giles, Cheryl, and Willa Miller, eds. *Arts of Contemplative Care: Pioneering Voices in Buddhist Chaplaincy and Pastoral Work*. Somerville, MA: Wisdom Publications, 2012.

Guth, Dana. 'Tufts among the First Universities to Establish Humanist Position in Chaplaincy." *Tufts Daily*, Sep 2, 2014.

Haederle, Michael. "College Buddhists on Campus." *Tricycle*, Fall 2020.

Hartford Seminary Islamic Chaplaincy. https://www.hartsem.edu/academics/degree-programs/islamic-chaplaincy.

Harvard Buddhist Community at HDS. "Third Annual Conference on Buddhism and Race." http://www.buddhismandrace.org.

Humanist Chaplaincy at Harvard and MIT. https://www.humanisthub.org.

Humanist Society. "Humanist Chaplains." https://www.theHumanistsociety.org/chaplains/apply.

Jacobsen, Douglas, and Rhonda Jacobsen. *No Longer Invisible: Religion in University Education*. Oxford: Oxford University Press, 2012.

Bibliography

———. *The American University in a Postsecular Age*. Oxford: Oxford University Press, 2008.

Kappler, Suzanne. "Chaplain Recalls Path to Making History." *Fort Jackson Leader*, Jun 12, 2009. https://www.army.mil/article/22584/chaplain_recalls_path_to_making_history.

Kazanjian, Victor H., Jr., and Peter L. Laurence, eds. *Education as Transformation: Religious Pluralism, Spirituality, and a New Vision for Higher Education in America*. New York: Peter Lang, 2000.

———. "The Journey Toward Multi-Faith Community on Campus: The Religious and Spiritual Life Program at Wellesley College." *Journal of College and Character* 9.2 (2007).

Knitter, Paul F. *Introducing Theologies of Religions*. Maryknoll, NY: Orbis, 2002.

Kujawa-Holbrook, Sheryl. *Injustice and the Care of Souls: Taking Oppression Seriously in Pastoral Care*. New York: Fortress, 2009.

Marquand, Bryan. "Thomas Ferrick, 84; Harvard's First Humanist Chaplain." *Boston Globe*, Jan 23, 2014. https://www.bostonglobe.com/metro/2014/01/23/thomas-ferrick-harvard-first-humanist-chaplain/9FTFMZuvwTVVnOEQAoyOpL/story.html.

Maxwell, Joseph A. *Qualitative Research Design: An Interactive Approach*. Thousand Oaks, CA: Sage, 2005.

MIT Spiritual Support. "Swami Tyagananda." https://studentlife.mit.edu/rl/who-we-are/swami-tyagananda.

Mitchell, Stephanie. "Harvard Appoints Muslim Chaplain." *Harvard Gazette*, Jun 21, 2017.

Molina, Alejandra. "Black Skeptics Find Meaning in Uplifting Their Community Through Social Justice." *Religion News Service*, Oct 15, 2020. https://religionnews.com/2020/10/15/3856053.

Morrongiello, Gabriella. "First of Its Kind: Tufts University Hires Humanist Chaplain for Atheist Students." *Daily Signal*, Sep 25, 2014. https://www.dailysignal.com/2014/09/25/first-kind-tufts-university-hires-humanist-chaplain-atheist-students.

Muslim American Society. "Muslim Chaplain at Howard University Resigns After 20 Years' Service." Harvard Pluralism Project, Apr 28, 2005.

Muslim Students Association National. https://www.msanational.org.

McGonigle, Gregory W. "*A Lively Experiment: World Religions in Rhode Island*." Harvard Pluralism Project. https://www.flickr.com/photos/pluralismproject/albums/72157654476411215.

———. "World Religions in Rhode Island." MDiv thesis, Harvard Divinity School, 2004.

Owens, Rod. *Love and Rage: The Path of Liberation Through Anger*. Berkeley, CA: North Atlantic Books, 2020.

Parks, Sharon Daloz. *Big Questions, Worthy Dreams: Mentoring Young Adults in Their Search for Meaning Purpose, and Faith*. San Francisco: Jossey-Bass, 2011.

Patel, Eboo. *Acts of Faith: The Story of an American Muslim, the Struggle for the Soul of a Generation*. Boston: Beacon, 2010.

———. *Interfaith Leadership: A Primer*. Boston: Beacon, 2016.

———. *Sacred Ground: Pluralism, Prejudice, and the Promise of America*. Boston: Beacon, 2013.

Bibliography

Pelletier, Rodney. "Georgetown Appoints Hindu Chaplain." *Church Militant*, Aug 11, 2016. https://www.churchmilitant.com/news/article/catholic-university-appoints-hindu-priest-as-chaplain.

Pew Research Center. "Demographic Portrait of Muslim Americans." Jul 26, 2017. https://www.pewforum.org/2017/07/26/demographic-portrait-of-muslim-americans.

———. "In U.S., Decline of Christianity Continues at Rapid Pace." Oct 17, 2019. https://www.pewforum.org/2019/10/17/in-u-s-decline-of-christianity-continues-at-rapid-pace.

———. "Muslims and Islam: Key Findings in the U.S. and Around the World." Aug 9, 2017. https://www.pewresearch.org/fact-tank/2017/08/09/muslims-and-islam-key-findings-in-the-u-s-and-around-the-world.

Pluralism Project. "Buddhism in America." https://pluralism.org/buddhism-in-america.

———. "Providence Zen Center." Published July 12, 2002; accessed December 8, 2020. https://hwpi.harvard.edu/pluralismarchive/providence-zen-center-diamond-hill-zen-monastery.

Prothero, Stephen. *Religious Literacy: What Every American Needs to Know—And Doesn't*. San Francisco: HarperOne, 2008.

———. *God Is Not One: The Eight Rival Religions that Run the World*. San Francisco: HarperOne, 2011.

Rossano, Cynthia Wight. *Durable Values: Selected Writings of Peter J. Gomes*. North Andover, MA: Flagship, 2012.

Ryan, Gery, and H. Russell Bernard. "Techniques to Identify Themes in Qualitative Data." *Field Methods* (Feb 1, 2003) 85–109.

Saldana, Johnny. *The Coding Manual for Qualitative Researchers*. London: Sage, 2009.

Secular Students Alliance. https://secularstudents.org.

Shipman, Asha. "Hindu Chaplaincy in U.S. Higher Education: Summary and Guidelines." *Journal of Interreligious Studies* 31 (2020) 21–36.

Silverman, Aaron Heshel. "At the University of Southern California a Humanist Chaplain Takes the Lead." *The Humanist*, Sep 5, 2017. https://theHumanist.com/features/interviews/university-southern-california-Humanist-chaplain-takes-lead.

Smith, Jane I. *Islam in America*. New York: Columbia University Press, 2009.

Stanford, Julianne. "Tufts Puts 'Humanist' Chaplain on Its Own Payroll, First in America." *College Fix*, Sep 22, 2014. https://www.thecollegefix.com/tufts-puts-humanist-chaplain-on-its-own-payroll-first-in-america.

Stedman, Chris. "After Atheists Asked, Tufts Creates First University-funded Humanist Position." *Religion News Service*, Sep 3, 2014. https://religionnews.com/2014/09/03/atheists-asked-tufts-creates-first-university-funded-humanist-position.

———. *Faitheist: How an Atheist Found Common Ground with the Religious*. Boston: Beacon, 2013.

———. *IRL: Finding Realness, Meaning, and Belonging in Our Digital Lives*. Minneapolis, MN: Broadleaf, 2020.

Sutton, Nicholas, et al. *Hindu Chaplaincy: The Oxford Centre for Hindu Studies Guide*. Oxford: Oxford Centre for Hindu Studies, 2017.

Ter Kuile, Casper. *The Power of Ritual: Turning Everyday Activities into Soulful Practices*. San Francisco: HarperOne, 2020.

University of Southern California. "USC Makes Historic Appointment of Hindu as Dean of Religious Life." *News Wise*, May 14, 2008.

Bibliography

Walker, Alyssa. "Georgetown University Hires Hindu Priest as Chaplain." Keystone Academic Solutions, Sep 22, 2016.

White, Stephen L. *The College Chaplain: A Practical Guide to Campus Ministry*. Cleveland, OH: Pilgrim, 2005.

Williams, Raymond Brady. *Religions of Immigrants from India and Pakistan: New Threads in the American Tapestry*. Cambridge: Cambridge University Press, 1988.

Yale University. "Muslim Life at Yale." https://muslimlife.yale.edu/history.

Yetunde, Pamela, and Cheryl A Giles, eds. *Black and Buddhist: What Buddhism Can Teach Us about Race, Resilience, Transformation, and Freedom*. Boulder, CO: Shambala, 2020.

Zauzmer, Julie. "Georgetown, a Jesuit University Is the First College with a Hindu Priest as a Chaplain" *Washington Post*, Aug 30, 2016.

Index

Adler, Felix, 85
adversity, 81–82
American Humanist Association, 89, 101, 104, 114
Asian American Cultural Center, 46
Association for Chaplaincy and Spiritual Life in Higher Education (ACSLHE), 8
Association of Muslim Chaplains, 16
Astin, Alexander, 122
Astin, Helen, 122
Augsburg University, 88, 98

Baha'i community, 73
Bailes, John, 55, 57–58, 59, 61–62, 66, 67, 69–71, 73, 74, 80–82, 83–84, 125
Bajwa, Omer, 11–12, 15, 16–17, 19–21, 26, 29, 125
Baloch, Naila, 15
Bell, Ryan, 95–96, 101–3, 105, 106, 109, 110, 112, 113–14, 125
Black Buddhists, 80
Black Lives Matter, 105
Black Theology Bible study, 4
Boston Area Rape Crisis Center (BARCC), 99
Boston Vedanta Society, 30
Bristol, Walker, 87, 88, 89, 92, 93–95, 99–100, 105–7, 108, 110, 112, 126
Brown Multifaith Council, 2
Brown University, 1–2, 12

Buddha Day celebration (Tufts University), 65
Buddhism, 53, 71, 77, 78–79
Buddhist chaplaincy
   accessibility of, 69
   accommodations for, 121
   challenges of, 72–80
   events in, 65
   future of, 80–84
   history of, 53–58
   Koru [Mindfulness] in, 69–71
   pastoral care in, 68–69
   preparation for, 58–62
   responsibilities of, 62–71
   robe of, 61–62
   scared space for, 75–76
   visibility of, 73
   wages of, 72
Buddhist Chaplaincy Initiative (Harvard Divinity School), 55–56

Campolo, Bart, 95
Catholicism, statistics regarding, 106
Chander, Vineet, 30, 31–34, 38, 43–45, 46–47, 49–50, 51, 125
chaplaincy
   accommodations for, 121
   arts of ministry of, 92, 120
   challenges of, 121–22
   changing landscape regarding, 3–6
   community care and, 42

Index

chaplaincy (*continued*)
   compassionate caring in, 34
   core elements of, 121
   diversification of, 122
   as evolving, 34
   growth of, 120
   hospitality of, 111–12
   identities of, 21–22
   pastoral care in, 92, 99
   roles and responsibilities of, 23–24, 34
   surveying the field of, 7–8
   as threshold keepers, 51–52
   training for, 120–21
   See also specific types
Chapman Walsh, Diana, 11
Christianity, statistics regarding, 106
Clinical Pastoral Education (CPE), 92
College Buddhism, 63–64
colonialism, 47–48
Columbia University, 31, 54, 55, 68, 71, 76, 89
community care, through chaplaincy, 42
Cooper Nelson, Janet, 2, 123
Cornell University, 12
COVID-19 pandemic, effects of, 39–40
Croft, James, 87
cultural appropriation, 47–48
cultural values, challenges to, 21

Dartmouth College, 85
Death Café (Tufts University), 89, 100
Dennett, Daniel, 88
Dharm, Pratima, 31
dharma, 79
Dharmalaya (Georgetown University), 46
Dharmic Discussions (Yale University), 41
Dharmic Life program (Georgetown University), 46, 50–51
discomfort, 81–82
Duke University, 12

Eck, Diana, 2, 119

Emerson, Ralph Waldo, 1, 53
Emory Buddhist Club, 58–59
Emory University, 31, 54
EnAct, 67
Epstein, Greg, 85, 86, 91, 92, 94, 96–99, 107–8, 109–10, 113, 114–15, 126
Ethical Culture Society, 87
Extinction Rebellion, 67

Ferrick, Tom, 85–86, 97
Figdor, John, 87
Flower Sunday (Wellesley College), 66

Georgetown University, 11, 31, 34–35, 46, 50–51
George Washington (GW) University, 32–33
Gomes, Peter J., 123
Gomez Brake, Vanessa, 89, 115–17, 125
Graduate Theological Union, 37

Harvard Community of Humanists, Atheists, and Agnostics (HCAA) (Harvard University), 96
Harvard Divinity School, 37, 54, 55–56, 60–61
Harvard University, 12, 30, 86, 96
Hijabfest (Howard University), 18
Hindu chaplaincy
   accommodations for, 121
   challenges of, 44–49
   future of, 49–52
   history of, 30–35
   office hours and, 45
   preparation for, 35–37
   responsibilities of, 37–44
   travel experiences and, 50
   wages of, 48–49
Hindu Students Council programs, 37–38
Hosein, Shareda, 15
hospitality, 40–41
Howard University, 11, 14, 17–18

Index

Humanism, 5, 6, 101–2, 106, 108, 112–13, 114–15, 116–17
Humanist chaplaincy
  activism and, 97
  challenges of, 101–6
  charitable projects in, 97
  community-building in, 103
  discrimination and, 105–6
  funding for, 109
  future of, 106–18
  growth of, 106–7
  history of, 85–90
  marketing challenge of, 102
  pastoral care in, 92, 99
  preparation for, 90–95
  program development and, 92
  program support through, 89, 100
  resources for, 105
  responsibilities of, 95–101
  wages of, 90, 94, 104
Humanist Hub, 86–88, 97
Humanist Society, 93–94
Hutchinson, Sikivu, 114

Ibrahim, Celene, 14, 15, 16, 17, 18–19, 22–23, 24, 26–27, 125
Immigrations and Naturalization Act, 53
Interfaith Student Council (Oberlin College), 4
Interfaith Youth Core, 3–4
Islam, growth of, 24–25

Jacobsen, Douglas, 119
Jacobsen, Rhonda, 119
Jainism, 50–51

Kazanjian, Victor, 11
Koru [Mindfulness], 69–71
Kugler, Sharon, 14, 40
Kwan Um School of Zen, 53–54

Lamont, Corliss, 85–86
LGBTQIA community, 60
Lindholm, Jennifer, 122
Loeb, John L., 86

loneliness, 103
Lytton, Nina, 87

Malcolm X, 11
Massachusetts Institute of Technology (MIT), 30
Mattson, Ingrid, 22
McLennan, Scotty, 4
meditation practices, 69–71, 76–77, 81–82
mental health care, 41–42
mindfulness practices, 76–77, 82
moral leadership, 20
Muhammad, Nisa, 14, 15–16, 17, 22, 27, 28, 29, 125
Muslim chaplaincy
  accommodations for, 121
  benefits of, 25–26
  challenges of, 20–24
  events of, 19–20
  funding for, 110
  future of, 24–29
  history of, 11–15
  identities in, 21–22
  partnerships of, 18–19
  preparation for, 15–17
  responsibilities of, 17–20
  social and moral development in, 19–20
  stereotypes and, 27–29
  support for, 26
  wages of, 23–24
Muslim Students Association (Tufts University), 18, 23

Naropa Institute, 54
New York University (NYU), 12, 31, 55, 60, 68, 71, 82, 89
North American Hindu Chaplains Association (NAHCA), 36, 121
Northwestern University, 12

Obama, Barack, 4
Owens, Rod, 79, 80, 125
Oxford Centre for Hindu Studies, 37

Index

Park, Doyeon, 54, 59, 60, 66, 68, 71, 72, 75–77, 78–79, 82, 83, 125
Patel, Eboo, 3–4, 87, 120
peace, 81
physical education, 57
Pluralism Project, 2
postcolonialism, 51–52
Princeton University, 12, 30, 33–34, 43–44, 46–47, 50, 51
Priya Rakkhit Sraman, 56
Prothero, Stephen, 120
Pruden, Leo, 53

Ramadan, 19–20
religious life departments, models of, 13
religious pluralism, 2
residential housing, challenges of, 21
Richardson, Bernard, 14
Rutgers University, 89

sacred space, importance of, 75–76
Sahn, Seung, 53–54
Schempp, Ellery, 88
"The Search for Meaning" course (Augsburg University), 98–99
secular sangha, 116
Secular Students Alliance, 89, 96, 105
Secular Students Fellowship (USC), 95
September 11, 2001 attacks, 11–12, 19, 33, 120
Sharan, Vrajvihari, 31, 34–35, 37, 42, 46, 47–49, 50–52, 125
Shipman, Asha, 31, 34, 36, 37–41, 42–43, 46, 47, 48, 50, 51, 125
Sikh Awareness Days (Princeton University), 51
Sikhism, 50–51
sleep, 70–71
Soni, Varun, 30–31
Sraman, Upali, 55–56, 58–59, 60–61, 63–64, 65–67, 68–69, 71, 72–73, 74–75, 77, 80, 82, 84, 125
Stanford University, 89

Stedman, Chris, 86, 87–88, 91, 92, 93, 98, 103–4, 108, 110–11, 126
Steinwert, Tiffany, 57
suicide, 112
sympathetic nervous system, 70

ter Kuile, Casper, 86–87
"This I Believe" series, 111
Thoreau, Henry David, 1, 53
Thurman, Howard, 14
Tufts Buddhist Mindfulness Sangha meditation community, 4
Tufts Freethought Society (Tufts University), 4, 88, 89, 99
Tufts University, 4, 12, 14–15, 18–19, 23, 31, 54, 55–56, 65, 73, 88–89, 99–101, 107
Tyagananda, Swami, 30

Union Theological Seminary, 54
University of California Davis (UC Davis), 3
University of Humanist Studies, 89
University of Massachusetts Boston, 103
University of Minnesota, 103
University of Southern California (USC), 30–31, 89, 95, 117
University of the West, 54

Vedanta Society, 30
Vesak Day, 65
Vivekananda, Swami, 30

Wellesley College, 11, 54, 56–57, 66, 69

Yale Divinity School, 46
Yale Humanist Community, 88
Yale University, 12, 14, 19–20, 31, 34, 38–40, 51, 88, 104
yoga, 47–48

Zoltan, Vanessa, 86–87

www.ingramcontent.com/pod-product-compliance
Lightning Source LLC
Chambersburg PA
CBHW070913160426
43193CB00011B/1447